Praise for *Every Natural Fact*

"What makes this book such a rnon-human
are kept in perfect balance: the   d son, with
all its funny, touching, realistic   to be
opened up to the mystery and ra   _. it is a splendid
fusion, as much about parenting   ..ı and generation gaps as it is
about patient observation of landscapes in flux. Jenkins' polished literary style
makes it, sentence by sentence, a joy to read."
> —Phillip Lopate, author of *Waterfront* and *At the End of the Day*

"Braiding together history, memoir, gentle parenting guidance, and superb
nature writing, Jenkins' prose illuminates the details of ordinary life."
> —Susan Cheever, author of *Home Before Dark* and *American Bloomsbury*

"Amy Lou Jenkins writes with complexity about the dance human beings do
with nature, and with one another...She puts together pieces of history, natural
history, and parenting to make a touching and memorable whole. The whole
thing rings true."
> —Michael Finley, judge of the Ellis/Henderson Outdoor Writing Award

"Her vivid imagery mixes a naturalist's precision with a spiritual seeker's poetry."
> —Robert Wake, author and editor of Cambridge Book Review Press and
> co-judge for the X.J. Kennedy Award for Nonfiction

"Armed with a keen sense of geography, geology, and biology—as well as a
delightful arsenal of regional folklore—Amy Lou Jenkins chronicles a series of
Wisconsin nature walks with her adolescent son, determined to face her own
foibles and learning to accept that DJ will eventually leave her loving nest. In
her cogent, smart book she holds on to her boy even as she lets him go, and
in the process discovers—through the natural world, through her faith, and
through guides such as Muir and Leopold—her own strength and vulnerability
as a mother."
> —Debra Gwartney, author of *Live Through This: A Mother's Memoir of
> Runaway Daughters and Reclaimed Love* and co-editor of *Home
> Ground: Language for an American Landscape*

EVERY NATURAL FACT
FIVE SEASONS OF OPEN-AIR PARENTING

AMY LOU JENKINS

EVERY NATURAL FACT

FIVE SEASONS OF OPEN-AIR PARENTING

AMY LOU JENKINS

HOLY COW! PRESS ★ DULUTH, MINNESOTA ★ 2010

Text, copyright © 2010 by Amy Lou Jenkins.
Cover and text design by Clarity (Duluth, Minnesota).
All rights reserved. Printed in the United States of America.
First printing, 2010
10 9 8 7 6 5 4 3 2 1
ISBN 978-0-9823545-1-3
Library of Congress Cataloging-in-Publication Data
Jenkins, Amy Lou, 1959-
Every natural fact : five seasons of open-air parenting / Amy Lou Jenkins.
    p. cm.
ISBN 978-0-9823545-1-3 (alk. paper)
1. Parenting—Anecdotes. 2. Mothers and sons—Anecdotes.
3. Natural history—Wisconsin. I. Title.
HQ755.8.J45 2010
306.874'3092--dc22
[B] 2010005046
Holy Cow! Press books are supported in part by grant awards from the
Lenfestey Family Foundation, the Elmer L. and Eleanor J. Andersen Foundation,
and by gifts from generous individual donors.

Holy Cow! Press books are distributed to the trade by:
Consortium Book Sales & Distribution, c/o Perseus Distribution,
1094 Flex Drive, Jackson, Tennessee 38301
For personal inquiries, write to:
Holy Cow! Press, Post Office Box 3170, Mount Royal Station,
Duluth, Minnesota 55803
Please visit our website: www.holycowpress.org

Mixed Sources
Product group from well-managed
forests and other controlled sources
www.fsc.org Cert no. SW-COC-002283
© 1996 Forest Stewardship Council

CONTENTS

ACKNOWLEDGEMENTS

The journey to move my writing from the sideline to center field began while I was working as a nurse. The most common end-of-life advice bestowed implicitly and explicitly by the terminally ill was rooted in regret about abandoned hopes and dreams. My dying patients initiated this book. They made me consider what was essential about my work and my life.

My husband, parents, sister, friends, and children treated me as an esteemed writer even before I'd broken into print. Judy Bridges and the writers from Redbird Writing Studios, Marilyn L. Taylor, and the Council for Wisconsin writers, Anne O'Meara and the UWM Spring Writers Festival, Jo McReynolds Blochowiak and the Great Lakes Writers Workshop, Anne Bingham, Nina Leopold Bradley, Sheree Bykofsky, and Mary E. Flynn, have all contributed to an essential community of support. Jim Perlman and Holy Cow! Press have championed literature from the Midwest since 1977 and nurtured this book project for the last year. Thank you also to all those friends and supporters who go unnamed.

Alverno College rewired me, recalling for me an ardor for words and ideas that had been stifled. Bennington College flung me into Liam Rector's vortex of prose, verse, and intensity. Susan Cheever introduced me to a range, addiction, and love of literature, as she celebrated the relationship between a life of letters and living a passionate life. Bob Shacochis recognized the first forays into my subject matter as a potential book and helped me to shape the concept of *Every Natural Fact*. He also kicked my butt when the work fell short and explained precisely why some writing had literary merit and some did not yet meet the standard. He called for a higher level of generosity to the reader, less lyrically known as a rewrite. This was invaluable. Tom Bissell gave bigheartedly of his talent, criticism, and support. He evaluated each word I sent him with the care of a master artisan. Phillip Lopate, the quintessential New York writer, pulled out his figurative flannel shirt and went with me to the Wisconsin wilderness where he pressed me to also write for those who are seduced by words rather than nature.

This book became a reality thanks to The Mesa Refuge Writing Fellowship, Ellis/Henderson Outdoor Writing Award, *Florida Review* Nonfiction Prize, *Flint Hill Review's* Nonfiction Award, *Rosebud Magazine's* X.J. Kennedy Nonfiction Award, Wisconsin Regional Writers Association Jade Ring Award, *Literal Latté* Nonfiction Prize, and the Santa Fe Writers Literary Prize, which have supported and honored my work.

Finally, thanks to all who work to preserve, restore, and love every natural place.

Dedicated to Dylan—who walked with me.

BETWEEN LAND AND WATER

"Every natural fact is a symbol of some spiritual fact."
RALPH WALDO EMERSON

In early spring I discovered a longing for unplugged time with my nearly eleven-year-old son—no phones, computers, iPods, or video-games. DJ and I began our open-air walks. While we walked the natural areas of Wisconsin, he grew toward manhood, and I grew into middle age. At the beginning, before we planned regular outings, I was uncharacteristically whiney, mired in apprehensions that fermented within a two-week bout of lousy weather. As the weather shifted inclinations, each walk took on its own disposition, so that the nature of the landscape and the day shaped the issues that came to dominate our time together: time that felt unhurried, essential, and sacred.

Those who dwell in northern climates share a measure of pride in our bravado toward winter. Like many who live where the audacity of winter throws blockades before spring, I come from sturdy stock—farmers, hard workers, and football fans who drink cold beer at outdoor stadiums during frigid January playoff games. I'm not a woman who ties a sequined cardigan over my shoulders lest a draft should offend me. My dad always told my sister Julie and me, "You girls are tough." We believed him.

When I was single, a divorced mom, I shoveled deep snow from a long driveway with a bundled baby on my back, changed a tire in an ice storm, and repaired my furnace with a wrench in one hand and a home repair manual in the other while a wind-up swing tinked out a melody as it comforted my snow-suit clad Andrea. Today, life is softer for me. When the snow falls Paul, my husband of over 16 years, rises early to snow blow our drive before he heads off to work. I still shovel the light stuff. I'm not a wimp. Sometimes I clean my snow-covered windshield with my bare hands and wait until the temperature drops below twenty before I consider wearing a winter hat. I eagerly head outside in December to take pictures of tall grasses and trees when snow and ice decorate their dormancy. My Milwaukee neighbors and I bake apple and cherry pies from frozen fruit bought during summer jaunts to Wisconsin's Door County peninsula. When the snow cleanly blankets our hills and trees, the white slate provides a reprieve from outdoor chores, as it covers broken fences and the weeds we never got around to pulling. Wisconsin's beauty and opportunity for recreation draws scads of folks from Illinois, trailing snowmobiles instead of the boats they pulled in summer. They join us when winter woolies, sleds, and skis claim a prominence in our lives. We watch the crimson red of the cardinal deepen its shade against the stark snow and appreciate the junco's flash of black and white tail stripes as he excitedly migrates to share our winters. January's and February's nip both sting, but we accept it. In the middle of winter, we make peace with boots, gloves, and Polartec gear. We live in a community that expects the cold and knows how to dress for sledding parties followed by hot cocoa with marshmallows for the kids and the optional shot of peppermint schnapps for the grownups. We enjoy our fireplaces, hand-crocheted afghans, and baked chicken dinners, and as long as the oven's heated, we whip up batches of chocolate chip cookies and banana bread.

We enjoy winter, but about the middle of March, when the dirty snow matches the color of the sky, we pine for a lasting spring. When the tides of spring are segregated by sloppy gray days, I'm not the only one who feels a sluggish depression. Throughout the Midwest, April often gives us heavy clouds that seal out the sun and send cold, rough rains and hail. The rise in barometric pressure presses our heads down and curls our spines into giant commas as we wait for the warmth and sunshine we believe we deserve by virtue of having endured over five months of winter. Last April, the season carried more asperity than most of us could stand up to. Our sun-deprived complexions and furnace-dried skin weathered within the gloom of a cabin fever that followed us outdoors when we stepped under the low ceiling of gray clouds. We don't usually like to admit any resentment toward Wisconsin, and we roll our eyes at our Arizona and Florida relatives when they call from their lanais with sunny weather reports and sickening good cheer about not missing the snow and ice. Beneath the tone of their happy voices, I hear a judgment that we who dwell in Wisconsin are moronic or underprivileged. Every other month, we brag about our state and don't tolerate any denigration cast upon our cherished heartland. In April, we stand down.

When the evening weather report called for sun and warmth, I realized that although Paul had to work, DJ and I had the day off. I leaned on the doorframe of our family room and told him, "Find your hiking boots and go to bed early. Tomorrow we're getting up at sunrise to search for something green or spring-like."

DJ looked up from his videogame, accepting my declaration with a cheery "Okay" that made me hyper-aware of my negative thoughts.

The sun didn't shine the next morning, but the haze carried more warmth than we'd felt for months. The temperature was expected to hit sixty-five degrees. A slight smile curled DJ's mouth as I gripped his shoulders while he feigned a walking sleep. I steered him toward the front passenger seat. Sitting next to the driver was still a novelty for him. Paul and I had made him wait until he weighed over ninety pounds before he could ride up front. He buckled his seatbelt, wadded his sweatshirt into a makeshift pillow, and leaned against the window.

A ball of fuzzy daylight illuminated the horizon as we left our neighborhood of pulled curtains and empty streets. Horicon Marsh, the largest freshwater cattail marsh in the United States, covering more than 32,000 acres, was an hour's drive away. In our migration there, we joined millions of birds. Over 60 percent of avian species in North America have a presence in this hot spot of the Mississippi flyway zone. Almost every type of waterfowl using the corridor rest, nest, or live at Horicon Marsh. The ancient flyway has been imbedded in birds' and butterflies' migration patterns since the glaciers began to recede, leaving behind ridged hills called drumlins, small hollows called kettles, and thousands of larger depressions we know as lakes and marshes. The flyway is so old that naturalists studying the migration of monarch butterflies over Lake Superior can only explain a consistent and distinct detour they make over a wide section of lake as the pathway developed when a glacial iceberg presented an obstacle to their travels.

DJ's mouth hung open, and his head bobbed as he slept. When the car veered toward Highway 45, his head rolled and jerked him awake. He looked around at the brown fields and gray skies. "The sun's not out? Isn't it supposed to be a nice spring day today?"

Instead of offering him encouragement about how warm weather was right around the corner, I supplied an exaggeration of commiseration. I told him about how, in the eighties, before we had a roofed baseball stadium, the Brewers had to change the date of their home opener twice in one year because of April snow. And when I married my previous husband on April 2, the forecast called for a mild day. Hail, instead of rice, pelted the wedding party when we raced to our cars after the ceremony. About a third of the guests and one of the band members in the Lockwood Trio missed the reception on account of the ice storm. The duo lacked harmony, which was a harbinger of a dissonant marriage. I didn't share information with DJ, but it was difficult not to recall the control, the slaps, and the desperate unhappiness of being married to a man who believed he loved me, yet sought to control me using multiple forms of intimidation. The hitting was kind of gift, as it awakened me to his desperate need to dominate. As soon as I recognized the violence hovering around Andrea, I left.

DJ leaned away from me and pressed his head against his sweatshirt. He closed his eyes as if he were unwilling to add my wintry discontent to his own.

I spoke softly, more as a reminder to myself than to my wisely disengaged son. "Sorry, DJ."

My son, my youngest child, sat in the passenger seat next to me reaching into his mouth, wiggling a loose incisor, and growing toward adolescence and manhood. Ever since he began to speak, he's always been a chatterbox, blabbing in the car about his favorite Sponge Bob cartoon, sharing each unfiltered thought that came into his head, and recounting the details of all the moments we spent apart; but recently a more laconic side of his personality had emerged. Like his father, his default description of each day was "Fine." He didn't want to talk about the "health lecture" at school, but he listened in exasperated quietness as Paul and I reviewed the basics of sexual maturation. DJ avoided me the rest of that evening, hyper-aware of our differences. The subject of the distinctions between men and women had come up before.

When DJ was about five, we read the book *I'm Lost* by Elizabeth Crary. The book instructs, "When lost, go to a police officer, a store clerk, or a woman with children—a mommy." Shortly after reading the book, a school program gave DJ the same advice, and later we saw a news segment that claimed that 77 percent of violent crime is attributable to men.

DJ took all this in and asked, "Are women nicer than men?"

I wouldn't believe that my son was destined to be mean, yet I couldn't say if I was being truthful about men in general when I answered "No."

The theme of *I'm Lost* (and the subsequent discomfort) had lain dormant in my memory for years. That unease had reanimated during this spring's cleaning bout when I placed the book into a Goodwill box. I was about to seal up the carton and put the thoughts away, but instead, I picked up the paperback and walked to DJ's room. We reviewed a PG-13 version of the be-careful lesson once again.

The town of Horicon seemed to still be asleep except for a fast food restaurant. I tapped DJ's leg. "Do you want some food before we get to the marsh?"

DJ sat up, looked right and left, laid his head back down, and ignored my question. "It still looks lousy outside. Isn't April weather supposed to be nicer than March?"

The last few days of March had teased us and sent some fifty-degree days to make us sweat in our winter clothes. March used the heavy dampness of our own bodies to cajole us into abandoning our down-filled ski coats and putting away the warm hats that flattened our hair. We even moved the high-traction boots (which were certified to twenty below zero) to the back of the closet. Then, April knocked us on our keisters by dumping an ice storm onto our bare heads and slick new Easter shoes.

The ground was still with littered broken branches from the April storm when I'd stepped out of the front door in my blue terry bathrobe to retrieve the morning paper last week. I'd found myself wandering my suburban yard, searching for green spikes on bulbs. My bare fingers dug through the frosty leaf mulch trying to find signs of impending relief from brown and gray. The tips of daffodils and small bulges that promised a bloom offered a slight textual reward for my iced fingertips, but I needed more. Paul walked out looking for me or the paper and stared at his brown lawn while I squatted and poked in my frozen flowerbed.

"It'll be green soon." He tried to sound optimistic, but then he looked up to the dark sky, shivered, hugged his arms against his chest, and added, "If it doesn't snow."

I lifted my face to him. "I've had enough." My bones felt cold; I hadn't seen our neighbors since we were shoveling after the last snowstorm, and even then I only saw the middle of their faces as they complained from beneath their woolen scarves about the return of winter. I was tired of the weight of winter clothes and winter pounds. The trees had been bare for six months. Piled on top of all this dismay, my grown daughter Andrea had moved out and left me oh-so-second-fiddle to the man of her life, as it should be. It was time, but she left me outnumbered in my home. Paul and DJ reminded me of my minority status when we voted on Friday night movies; they wanted an action flick, overruling my pick, a quirky independent film. When it came to where to go for dinner, they vetoed Thai food in favor of burgers. I stood my ground even without my daughter's vote and forbade the ash-colored paint that my son and husband suggested as a good color for the hallway.

When the daffodils finally broke their winter dormancy and pushed up inches of green spikes of promise, my guys inadvertently stepped on them and smashed the only tiny slashes of spring in the flower garden. I interpreted their destructive behavior as if it were emblematic of the degradation of our planet under the leadership of the world's paternalistic societies. They were sorry; I was sullen. In my climate-induced gloom, I began to ruminate.

A newspaper story, with photos of nurses in wedding gowns who protested hospital management, reminded me of my personal career injustices. A hospital conglomerate had recently decreased health benefits for nurses, citing that the women could use their husband's insurance. This isn't true in our household, as my husband's small business insurance is expensive and provides spotty coverage. We manage to get sick and injured in non-coverable ways. When I was a divorced mom and nurse, providing health insurance for my daughter, my lousy HMO benefits took almost a fourth of my take-home pay. In Wisconsin, almost 30 percent of all homes are single-parent households, and over 80 percent of these are headed by women. The national trends are similar. Problems concentrate in Milwaukee, where a third of all children live in poverty. Most poor children do not have an employed father. Medicaid covers many children's basic health needs, but those who live slightly above the official poverty level, because of earned income, don't qualify. Women still earn less than men for comparable jobs, seventy-seven cents on the dollar, and they bear a heavier burden when it comes to household work and child rearing. The differences between being a man and being a woman isn't just biologic, it's usually economic. A society that places women as helpmates and second-income wage earners engenders suffering for women and the children they support.

As I considered my daughter going off on her own, with plans for career, marriage, and children, I worried that her gender might affect her economic future and therefore become a source of pain and suffering. The men in our lives bore no specific blame that I could pinpoint. Andrea's fiancé has given her years of loving boyfriend credibility, and my Paul rates as a sweetheart a large percentage of the time, but less than half of all marriages are successful in raising children in the original two-parent household. The general culture still blunts the potential of females with notions of women as helpmates. I knew from experience how tough life can be for a single mom. I was in a funk, missing my daughter and awfulizing that the worst of the past might predict her future.

DJ and I drove past the north-flowing Rock River that supplies the marsh and entered the parking lot with access to the National Wildlife Refuge. The road to the marsh boardwalk opened on April 15. Since it was April 14, we had to hike in.

I hoped if we witnessed a flurry of wildlife migrating back to our Wisconsin version of spring, it would improve my attitude. We started through a dormant brown prairie. DJ carried the backpack. Alongside the road, I spied the diminutive first petals of the common mullein. I knelt and touched its leaves. "Feel how soft and woolly they are."

DJ complied. "Yeah," he said, barely opening his mouth. "Soft. Woolly."

I looked at him while rubbing the foliage. "I'm going to teach you something that I know you will use at some time in your life, okay? The mullein can grow to over ten feet with a long club of yellow flowers that blooms all summer. They tend to grow in sunny spots at the edges of woods or swamps. These base leaves will grow to over a foot long. They're easy to spot. You won't find them in the woods. Listen up; here's the important part. If you think you're going to have to do a Number Two in the woods, take a few large leaves from the base of the mullein. It won't hurt the plant. They are softer than flannel, tougher than TP, and non-irritating. You've got to think ahead, because once you head into the woods for privacy, you won't find this plant."

DJ sneered. "Did you really have to tell me that?"

"I thought it was gross when Grandpa Ed taught me, but twenty years later while camping on an island in the Menomonee River, I was very happy he did. Feel this. Softer than Charmin!"

We walked on. The air carried a fresh green smell, like asparagus cooking. DJ began to sing:

"I have a magic toenail.

I keep it on my foot.

It's always there to cheer me up

When things just go ker-plunk."

When I asked him if he might get into nature mode, he sang more softly. "Look," I told him, "if we are quiet and watchful, I know we'll see something wonderful. We haven't seen anyone on this trail, so the only people here to scare the wildlife are you and me. Let's be quiet."

He believed me, and we slowed our pace. I watched his freckled face as his dark blue eyes scanned the terrain. Prairie changed to marsh around a curve in our path. I stopped, grabbed his shoulder, stood behind him, and pressed my cheek to his dark brown hair. Trying to match his line of sight with my arm, I pointed to a five-foot tall bird ahead of us in a stand of bare scrub trees. "Sandhill crane," I whispered.

DJ got out the binoculars and the *Peterson Field Guide*. "He's as tall as me." We were able to get within twenty feet. DJ hung the binoculars around his neck and looked back and forth from the picture in the book to the bird before us. We were still.

DJ whispered, "Gray with dark red around the eyes and head. Up to a seven-foot wingspread. Yup, it's a sandhill." He kept studying the bird, which now walked comfortably in our stillness as he pecked for food.

Sounds of the marsh grew louder. Crickets and leopard frogs buzzed and plucked. We saw a nearly fluorescent green water snake slither over the top of the thick, dark water. I noticed the tips of emerging vegetation. Cattails, marsh marigolds, arrowhead, and water lilies reached through the undulating watery mud toward the spring light. The muck bubbled and moved. In an instant, the sun came out. It must have been in a place like this, I thought, that Gerard Manley Hopkins conjured the lines:

"What is all this juice and this joy? A strain of the earth's sweet being in the beginning."

The exhalation of the swamp blew the gray lid off the spring day. We tied our sweatshirts around our waists, stood taller in the high sky, and continued on. Canada geese buzzed our heads as if we were approaching a landing strip. In the distance, they descended and dropped their feet before blending into a far woodland stand.

"What's up there?" DJ asked.

"A lot of open water and a floating boardwalk through the marsh."

DJ, who had taken the lead, stopped for a moment and looked back at me. "Let's be real quiet. We're the only ones here."

We stepped onto the wooden planks and adjusted our footing to the boardwalk's give and bounce in response to each of our steps. The ducks weren't nesting yet, so they floated around and mingled as if circulating at a crowded cocktail party. DJ kept the bird guide at his chest, looking to the water and then to the book. "That one's a redhead duck. What's next to it?"

"A coot."

"Oh, yeah, black with a white bill."

DJ counted a flock of thirty-eight blue winged teals as they circled twice in front of us flashing chalky azure wing patches. On the second pass, they flew close enough for us to confirm their white facial stripes and stippled brown and white bodies as they turned toward us in formation. We kept our eyes skyward and turned a shuffling half circle to watch them land behind us. They settled in coupled pairs, immediately blending with a flock of feeding pintails. We laughed with silent puffs of breath as they dunked, bottoms-up for submergent vegetation. The pairs, all in their own time, took turns. First the male stood watch while the female flashed her tail feathers; then the female stayed upright while the male tipped over to feed.

DJ pointed to a pair of ducks that looked a lot like the redhead, except that the drake's back was gray and his belly and sides were creamy white. "What are those?" he asked. But he paged through *Peterson's* for the answer, rather than looking to me, so I stayed quiet.

Each duck had a better chance of survival when it had a mate looking out for it. The survival of every species, at the most basic biologic level, depends on coupling.

—✦—

Looking back at my history of failed relationships, I realized that I've always been able to remember them in a way where I come off as the wronged-party—the good one. I had my justifications: a peeping Tom neighbor, a relative's roaming hands, hundreds of attempts to conquer me sexually with few attempts to know me. A male boss, no, there were more than one, made lascivious advances and punished my family-supporting career when I spoiled their fun.

Attention from husbands and boyfriends changed into a desire to possess and control me. That kind of love didn't satisfy; instead, it smothered me until I couldn't stand the burden of their overbearing company or until they moved on to another conquest. Eventually, I came to understand how I helped to establish those ill-fated relationships by deferring to those men. I let the volume in their voices overpower my inner voice, so that I couldn't even recognize my own thoughts. I thought that this was how a woman found love and security.

Historically, men have been the ones who fought for power, money, and resources. Perhaps I thought, long ago, that a man might grab some of those resources for me.

Between and after those ill-fated relationships, I'd put myself through college, bought my own home, and advanced from nurses' aide to director of a home health care agency. I gained professional skills that carried me beyond the parental advice I'd received that "Only ugly girls need college." I came to see that aggression steeped in egocentricity was hard to admire and impossible to live with—perhaps as difficult to weather as my passive-aggressive bouts of compliance followed by angry revolt. Once I'd been purged of most of my coquettish impulses (not only because I'd gotten smarter, but also because I just couldn't rely on youthful beauty because I was aging), Paul asked me out. He was a kind man—a doctor who practiced in the inner city. I had respected him for years before we began our five-year courtship. Only when I was sure that I didn't need a man, when I owned my independence, was I able to bring a whole person to a marriage. That sounds so obvious, but I don't think I'm the only woman who didn't understand her own abilities while very young and attractive and while her esteem was fed by the men who were happy to pay to possess their prize. It was easy to imagine that those men who competed to care for me and who showed off their cars and muscles and wallets could offer me security. Instead of sharing power, I submitted to support roles where my voice and talents were silenced and bound. When my relationships weren't built on the shoulders of two strong people, they crumbled.

Paul and I do jockey for control of our lives within our marriage. I never played the demure dependent with him, so I didn't feed his inherent tendency to dominate. And certainly, he is a man without a lot of the insecurities that create a need to subjugate another. He would, however, assume an excessive share of power in our relationship if I let him. We don't live our lives with our heads jutting from an evenly spaced yoke; everything is not equal. I hoped that DJ's witness to our respectful juggling of power would serve his future relationships.

Paul often offers suggestions about how I should do things. I do listen. Then, I consider my needs, his needs, and the family's needs. This list can not be permanently ordered; sometimes I come first; sometimes my needs come last. This is my choice. But he does not govern me anymore than I govern him. Once I placed my own needs as a priority in the relationship, I found a marriage that lasted, and our son knew a childhood with an intact family—a gift we hadn't given Paul's previous children nor mine.

Paul used to say he'd like to go with me on nature hikes, canoe rides, and camping trips. He asked me to wait for him, but accommodating his work and on-call schedule usually meant the outing never happened. I resented his job while I waited and imagined the trilliums on the forest floor, cranes nesting in the marsh, barn swallows swooping and flashing their iridescent feathers in streaks of sunlight, and morning frost settling on cedars. Once I started as a den leader for Cub scouts (about the time DJ became old enough to easily travel to undeveloped settings), I began a pattern of taking DJ to natural places. I learned to let Paul know he was welcome and then to pack up a backpack and DJ and go.

⟨✦⟩

DJ pointed to a picture of a duck in the field guide. "See? The canvasback has a bigger and darker bill than the redhead."

The drake's ruddy red head signaled mating season. He'd stay with his mate for now, but these males are known to take off during early incubation and find a molting lake. The females incubate and protect the eggs while the males go away during their ugly time of the year and return well fed and energized to help parent the ducklings. We were close enough to notice the wedged shape of their bills and the red eyes that reflected up to us from the calm water. They didn't dive for us, but these versatile ducks swim above and under water and are one of the fastest of all ducks on the wing. Suddenly the canvasbacks took off, beating their wings feverishly until they caught an air current which carried them out of sight.

Unfortunately for the canvasback, they are especially tasty. As a result, their population plummeted during the first third of the twentieth century. They rebounded a bit when commercial market hunting of ducks was outlawed, but loss of habitat and pollution-induced changes in marsh vegetation have kept their numbers low.

DJ thought the canvasbacks looked "tight." Those of us who are too old to be tight might have used the word "cool" or "lovely." He appreciated that the ducks always had this place to come to—a natural place. But Horicon hadn't always been available to the wetland breeders who flourished here for over 15,000 years before European settlers took the land from the Sauk. Referring to a tourist newspaper and tapping my memory, I explained the history to DJ.

Men fought bloody battles to take this land away from a tribe who came from an ancestry of people who lived as part of the ecosystem that flourished without any attempt to master or control the wetlands. Chief Black Hawk was the final Sauk leader to try to hold on the only life he knew by warring with the settlers. When he resigned himself to leaving his homeland in the 1830s, he said of the region, "Rock River was a beautiful county. I loved my towns, my cornfields, and the home of my people. I fought for it. It is now yours. Keep it as we did."

By 1846, the settlers had dammed the Rock River and turned the marsh into a fifty-square-mile lake, considered at the time to be the largest human-made lake in the world. Canvasbacks wouldn't have nested here then; they need reeds like cattails to support their green eggs in a nest of flattened rushes. Farmers thought they could drain their marsh water into the lake, turning wetland to agricultural land. They found that the peat and moisture in the soil prohibited the growth of any root crops, and overall yields were low. Bass, pike, pickerel, bullhead, and musky were so prolific in the lake that farmers were said to dip baskets into the lake and pull up enough fish to feed their pigs. DJ snorted when I told him that the meat from these Horicon pigs wasn't marketable; the pork tasted fishy. In 1869, hunters with little to shoot at, conservationists, and women's groups all spoke up about the immorality of the losses in bird and duck populations. The dam came down. Horicon Marsh didn't reappear as expected because the natural flooding systems, rivulets, land contours, and vegetation had been destroyed. Low water levels and exposed peat led to fires and more destruction. In 1930, after the legislature passed the Horicon Marsh Wildlife Refuge Bill, the State began to buy back more of the farmland and rebuild the Rock River Dam. They partially flooded the area to approximate the conditions existing before the meddling began. This natural marsh now requires constant vigilance, including managing water levels and burning the prairie in an attempt to mimic conditions that once came naturally to the water and land.

Over the next two hours we inched across the half-mile-long boardwalk. DJ identified each bird species we saw: grebes, mergansers, great blue herons, and more. Above us, flocks flew in and out of our vision. We tried to count V-formations, but they converged and separated so we could only tell that there were more than twenty-two flocks in our sight at one time. Most were a series of dots, but some would fly close and land on the open water near us. While DJ counted Canada Geese, I did not have to remind myself that this male, my son, should not be held accountable for all the paternalistic power gone awry in the bygone years of Horicon, the world, or my life. And if he is innocent, I conjectured, there must be others.

As soon as our feet crossed the threshold from boardwalk to trail, DJ announced, "I'm hungry." Within a quarter mile he began the "Magic Toenail" song again, this time sharing that Alec from Scouts had taught him the song. When he approached the trunk of a large bur oak lying across the trail, he fell silent.

"Over or around?" I asked, but he took a running start and leapt over it before I finished the question. I turned my back to the three-foot-wide trunk and sat down. "I can't jump as high as you can. Let me think about what to do."

DJ handed me a bottle of water and unwrapped the first of two granola bars he held in his hand. He sat next to me, facing the way we would go, while I faced the way we'd come.

Sitting with my hungry son reminded me of the day we missed our fish fry. It was during a vacation near Minocqua—a week of hiking, swimming, reading, and playing cards in a rustic cabin in the up-north Wisconsin woods. After about six days of togetherness, I was itchy to be alone and suggested I skip the Scheer's Lumberjack Show to browse antique stores. The lumberjack aficionados agreed, recognizing they would miss the drudgery of going antiquing with me. After I dropped them at the Scheer's grandstands, I drove out of town a few miles and back, just to enjoy my independence at the wheel. The touristy antique shops seemed too clean. Green paint on the handle of the potato ricer wasn't original, and the amber Globe fruit jar's clasp delivered a shine that could not have matched its age. Still, I enjoyed the search. By the second store, a shellacked log cabin that smelled of Pine Sol, a pattern emerged. Wives walked slowly, eyes intent on the shelves long after their husbands had tired of browsing remnants of country living and up-north tchotchkes.

The men wore similar uniforms: polo shirts and pleated khaki shorts. Hands in pockets, they looked awkward, as if too big to stand comfortably among cranberry glass, porcelain dolls, spindly-legged tables, and tea cups in the stuffed shops that played loon calls on CD (available, of course, for purchase). By the third store, I was in love with the uncomfortable patience of these men. If Paul had come, he would also have simulated interest and then resolved himself to waiting while I finished shopping for unnecessaries. I picked up Paul and DJ from the show with only a few dollars' worth of purchases but declared the shopping trip fun. The two-hour absence from my men and its revelations had sparked a renewed affection.

We cleaned up for dinner and were looking forward to the fish fry. On the way, the air stilled, and the clouds in the west grew heavy. From the lobby of The Pines Restaurant, we stole lusty glances into the dining room at the plates of golden-fried lake perch and walleye while the sky darkened and the wind rushed around the shiny log building and through the stands of straining trees. Thunder began to crack in the distance, and we heard the clouds dropping lakes of water on the roof and against the windows. Just as we were seated, the lights went out. The waitress carried a candle in a lantern over to us and said they would not be serving. She invited us to go down to the basement shelter until the storm passed. We should have been worried about the storm and the wind, but we were thinking of food.

The strong winds had diminished, but torrential rain drenched us as we hurried to the car by following a ray of light trembling from Paul's flashlight keychain. We couldn't find another restaurant. The storm had wiped out electricity everywhere. Lines of cars appeared at each road into the woods, and we didn't understand the traffic jams on all the back roads. We joined a stalled procession of cars on the road to our cabin and waited while trucks and cars got in line behind us and confirmed our decision to stay in line. The cars didn't move at all for about a half-hour, then we moved a quarter mile and stopped again. Men in khakis left their cars and walked ahead to check on the problem. Paul joined them. DJ and I stayed in the car and watched several ATVs roar by us on the shoulder of the road. We saw a pile of logs in a ditch and heard loud buzzing beyond our line of vision. Men with chainsaws hurried toward the action. DJ pressed his nose to the foggy car window and occasionally leaned back to wipe the condensation with his sleeve. Freshly drenched from the rain, Paul returned with dirty hands and clothes, explaining that trees were down all over the road. Many of the locals kept chainsaws in their trunks, so several men raced ahead to help clear logs, then hurried back to their cars to move ahead. They worked in warm, intermittently heavy rain. Paul brought news with each trip back to the car. "That one wasn't bad—a clump birch. The hickory was so big it crossed the road, grazed a house, and took out a shed."

DJ ate the chocolate-covered craisins from my shopping bag and the Mentos mints from my purse. He asked several times to go out with his dad to cut and move the trees, but with all the rain, chainsaws, and men working, we held him back. Eventually, he fell asleep.

I asked Paul If I should come out and help, but he said there were so many men at each felled tree that they had enough for an assembly line. "Stay here with DJ," he said, "and keep dry."

At one of the barricades the road looped around, and I could see the men at work and hear them through the slightly open window. They held their heads down when the rain intensified and wiped sheets of water from their faces with their palms. I heard a man in khaki shorts ask, "Why don't you take a break and let me cut with the chainsaw for a while?" He reached for the saw.

Another man held out his palm to stop him and cautioned, "He's been driving around with that chainsaw in his trunk since last Christmas waiting for a night like this. He sure as hell is not going to turn it over to you." Chainsaw envy, I thought.

When we finally returned to our cabin, it was after two in the morning, and we were famished. We still didn't have electricity, but our flashlight led us to candles. Since it was our final night in the cabin, we only had a few leftovers. Paul dried off and got DJ into pajamas while I threw on my robe and began to mince onion, garlic, and a few slices of ham. I fried it up on the gas stove, adding eggs and a huge portion of leftover spaghetti noodles from the night Paul had cooked. He always makes too many noodles, but we were happy to have them this time. I grated the last of the fresh Parmesan over the top. We raised one can of beer, one stem of wine, and one box of grape juice to toast our owl-light dinner.

"How'd you come up with this recipe?" Paul asked. "It's great."

DJ looked at the fried spaghetti with ham and eggs hesitantly, took a bite, and shook his head in an enthusiastic nod of approval.

I explained that fried spaghetti with ham and eggs was an Italian recipe I'd ordered in Florence at a restaurant where no one spoke English. I'd just pointed to the menu at something I could afford.

Paul complimented me with his mouth full. "I'm impressed."

I was impressed with him too. In fact, I was kind of turned on by the competence and camaraderie of all those men working and heaving those fallen trees. If I'd been in a line of cars with only women, I wanted to believe we could have handled the chainsaws and moved the logs, but we might not have been driving around with anticipatory longing and heavy equipment in the backs of our trucks. We might have had to cut the trees into shorter lengths before we could move them off the road. We would have congratulated ourselves and might have enjoyed the power of the chainsaws in our hands. But the noise of the saws and ATVs may have given me a headache, and my thighs chafe when I walk in wet slacks. I didn't think a group of my girlfriends could have made the best of a bad situation quite as well as those men did. They almost made it look fun. In truth, I didn't see one woman out in that storm. There is something in most men, though, that makes them feel good about protecting their families and using their brawn. That night, I liked it. Not because I was helpless without their intervention, but because it seemed an arduously purchased gift of love and protection.

I don't want to be told I can't use the chainsaw or that I'm always responsible for dinner, but that night, I appreciated being excused from the heavy work and then making an impressive meal. When I looked back at this stereotyped setting—him clearing the road, DJ watching, me cooking—my pleasure in the reminiscence did bother me. I had to remind myself that choosing to cook dinner for my hardworking husband did not make me a traitor to the feminist cause. The National Organization for Women will not revoke my membership if I'm spotted in an apron (let's not send them announcements, okay?). If men need to temper their aggressive proclivities, then women need to step out of their penchant to subvert themselves and instead bring all their talents and influences into play. DJ saw his dad and other assiduous men working in the rain without a complaint. It rained; the logs were heavy. Families were hungry and tired, as were the men. They joked and stayed focused on the job. They did everything but sing "Hi, ho, hi ho, it's off to work we go." DJ learned a lot that night about being a man. And that night, I enjoyed the adventure in cooking for my family.

In a culture where strong women may not have an equal share of power but are not likely to be tortured or killed for their assertive reach for shared governance of all societies' structures, I thought it an abdication of duty for women to remain submissive. Men can be harsher than women—even more dangerous. The asperity in their nature can lead to desecration, brutality, and war. But not that night. Their brutish force cleared the way for dozens of families to go home. My Paul seemed especially strong and tender as we both pushed through our exhaustion and found the energy to make love in a dark cabin in the north woods, just before a calm sunrise.

DJ finished his granola bars, but they didn't do the trick. He was ready for town and more substantial food. By the time I swung my legs around the trunk of the tree, he was way ahead. Where prairie met woodland, I could hear the liquid gurgling of red-winged blackbirds mixing with the soprano whistle of a cardinal and the chatter of the wren. I stopped, listened, and thought of Shelley's "To a Skylark":

> Teach me half the gladness
> That thy brain must know,
> Such harmonious madness
> From my lips would flow,
> The world should listen then, as I am listening now.

I knew my freshly sunny attitude had come by way of a temporal injection of spring. If the benevolent change in the season had directed my thoughts and memories away from enemizing the opposite sex, it seemed best to go with that renewal. My discontent (okay, hostility) would reappear, and I hoped that it would cycle back a bit more specifically directed to unjust acts rather than toward men in general. Since my son was growing toward manhood, I was compelled toward a reasoning compassion. DJ was about to complete grade school and enter the years of pulling away that I'd known with my daughter and still remembered from my own adolescence. I didn't want this change to happen behind the closed door of his bedroom.

DJ waited for me by pretending he'd fallen asleep leaning across the hood of the car. We bought sandwiches in the town of Mayfield and stopped at a small red barn just off Highway 22 to buy cheese curds. "Just made them this morning," the ruddy-faced man promised. He was in earnest, because they were still warm and squeaked against our teeth when we chewed them—a treat all our Arizona and Florida relatives had to do without.

DJ took a swig of root beer, letting it wash over a mouthful of cheese, and said, "We should do stuff like this more often."

I jumped on his suggestion. "Okay. Let's try for a trip once a month." I wanted to spend time with him in primary settings without civilized distractions—places where I believed life felt more original then virtual. When he was grown, I hoped we would both understand what it meant to become a man.

On the way home, when I suggested fried spaghetti for dinner, DJ asked if I would teach him to make it. While I told him I would, I noticed the chartreuse swells on the weeping whips of the willow and the lawns that had begun to green up in just one April day. DJ went back to wiggling his tooth. I knew we would eat fried spaghetti that night and share reminiscences of the big Wisconsin up-north storm, just as we do every time we repeat the menu. We would talk about the marsh and how difficult it had been for people to learn to live in partnership with all the complexities and dualities at the intersection of land and water. Contradictory elements converged: wet and dry, cold and warm, clouds and sunshine, masculine and feminine. Spring didn't just arrive in the reconditioned marsh; it seemed to originate within the alchemy of opposites. It came with the force of high waters behind a breaking ice dam and replaced the season of gray with a flourish of life.

Near our neighborhood, we saw a line of fifteen, DJ counted them, bicyclers in sleek yellow and black. Bare-kneed children played in front yards, on sidewalks, and at the park. At a lengthy red light, we stopped in front of a small blue house with a big picture window framed in white trim. The sidewalk and steps to the front porch were littered with chalk drawings, balls, a small yellow two-wheeler lying on its side, and a pile of plastic action figures. Inside, a little boy in white briefs flew into the air in front of the picture window with his arms and legs in spread-eagle position. He was jumping on a couch, probably breaking a household rule. Again and again he flew into the framed view of the picture window, waving his outstretched arms as he jumped. We felt his joy and wanted to stay and watch, but when the light turned green, it was time to move on. We left him in midair.

CLOSE TO HOME

"Gentile or Jew
O you who turn the wheel and look to windward,
Consider Phlebas, who was once handsome and tall as you."
T.S. ELIOT

D J spotted a deer trail that looked as if it led to the Menomonee River while I tried to think of a way to explain death. The space for my words imploded as my son moved away from me toward the passage through the trees. It is July 2, the date of a full moon in the month that Buddhists believe the dead return to visit the living.

This morning, only a few houses from our home on the way back from DJ's summer orchestra lesson, a buck with just an inch of antler crossed in front of our car, grabbing my line of sight with his intent dark eyes and reminding me that my eleven-year-old son and I were overdue for a nature outing. Nature came to get us. DJ claimed the buck stared directly into his eyes as he passed, but I swore he glared into mine and even turned his head back over his shoulder to maintain eye contact as he traveled from parkway to suburban lawn. His interest in us evaporated as his front hooves hit the curb. We kept watching him, unaccustomed to seeing a slow-moving deer so near. Usually they bolt across our road or stand statuesque for a moment before darting back into the veil of trees and shrubs. This buck seized our attention and then became oblivious to us, as if we didn't exist in the same dimension.

We saw the short spikes on his head that inspire the name of the July full moon in the *Farmers' Almanac*: the "full buck moon." This is the month the buck begins to re-grow antlers in preparation to fight, to the death if needed, for the right to mate. His coat was caramel with cream trim and scratched from shoulder to rear as if keyed by an angry hoodlum. He grazed on the neighbor's lawn, and she came out on the porch and sat on her step with her chin in her palm to watch.

On the strip of mowed parkway in front of the woods where the buck had emerged, a red-tailed hawk swooped down for a touch-and-go landing, sporting a squirming mole in its clutches. A poplar tree with stark white undersides of leaves winked in the light breeze.

At home, the morning paper headlined "Five US Servicemen Killed in Attack at Iraqi Base" and "White Pelican returns to Wisconsin as Mississippi Wetlands are Restored." And from the obituary page, "Beloved daughter departed this earth…born 1995." I didn't know this girl, but I scanned the death notices looking for a distance this "beloved daughter's" age withheld. Ninety-eight was comfortable, sixty-nine was so young, and the iniquitous reality of a teenager as a corpse unsettled me. Death sometimes tries to shove itself to center frame in my life; I push back.

I'd been away from home for almost two weeks as a part of a graduate program. When I'd left, DJ's voice seemed to play every sharp and flat note possible in the measure of one sentence, but when I returned, he spoke in a smooth, deep voice that I knew other women would come to love. On the day I returned from my residency in Vermont and drove to DJ's bus stop from day camp, I expected a gleeful look and a hungry hug when he spotted me as the pickup person. He saw me, but he looked away and didn't even bend to look in the car window. When he approached, I saw only his arm reaching for the handle and his blue Homer Simpson "This is your brain… on doughnuts" T-shirt. His greeting was a baritone, "Hi." Moments later, I could see only the back of his head because he looked out the window and away from me. A block later, on a quiet, anonymous street, I pulled the car over and hugged and kissed my acquiescent son.

The following day, as I tried to work at the computer, he lingered next to me, and when I draped my arm across his waist, he crawled into my embrace, and all five feet two and a half inches of him lingered in my lap.

In front of the window, a clattering of bikes and kids passed on the street that separates our house from the woods and river. He dropped, as if assault weapons were spraying the house with bullets. From the floor, my son inquired, "Anybody see me?"

"No one saw you hug your mom. They didn't even look." I closed the blinds and didn't get any work done while DJ told me about camp and complained about too many little girls in his horse-riding group.

Although DJ had seemed enthusiastic when he'd agreed to walk with me in our neighborhood woods, he raised his eyebrows as he saw me stuffing a backpack with bug repellant, water, and field guides to trees, birds, and wildflowers. The weight of my hiking boots reminded me that this neighborhood walk was different from my usual morning walking circuit. This was my opportunity to explore the areas I usually buzzed by while trying to keep my heart beating at 70 percent of my maximum rate. While swinging my arms and discussing kids and dinner plans with my walking girlfriend, I often looked at the trails, ponds, and bridges with longing and intention to come back for a better visit. The route was a rectangle with a river running in the middle and bridges at each end. Today, DJ and I were going inside the rectangle, something I hadn't done in almost two months.

DJ's eyes looked up at me, but his neck and shoulders tilted down. "Why are you bringing all those books and stuff just to walk across the street?"

"Don't worry. We won't be more than a few hours."

DJ's exploration with me was a gift he'd promised to give, and he didn't whine or try to beg his way out of it. Instead, he teased, and before we'd left the yard, he rapidly fired all the complaints he was too mature to say in earnest. "Are we almost home? How much further? I have to go to the bathroom." That done, he elbowed me and pointed across the street to bright orange blooms of summer.

The blossoms of the day lily species each last only one day and often bloom in succession. They are so prolific along roadsides that most folks call them ditch lilies. Six buds on a lily could mean that in six days, the flowers would be gone for a year. Negative thinking, I told myself. Something else will come into bloom when the prairie lilies are done, and more buds may form on these plants to bring more weeks of summer blossoms. It's only in July, though, that summer is this bold.

We crossed the black top road, and I silently recalled the mess we'd seen there on an evening dog walk last month. Perhaps DJ did too; his eyes focused on the same stretch of blacktop that revealed nothing of prior events, not even a faint stain. That night a possum lay split open on the street, and seven nubs of babies crossed the road ahead of the body, recreating an image of the impact. DJ had bent over one of the nubs, shook his head, and ticked the roof of his mouth. The mamma and her scattered pearls were gone by morning.

There's a man in Milwaukee who drives an old truck under contract with the county and picks up offensive refuse that can be handled by one man: dead dogs, bloated raccoon carcasses, and all manner of carrion and objects dumped on the street. I saw his picture in the paper a few autumns ago when he found a garbage bag holding a cold newborn baby with a smidgen of cry left in her. He called the Rescue Squad. She lived. I wonder if that man still considers that baby girl, in a warm home, her light brown hair grown in. She must be walking, already talking like crazy, now almost ready for kindergarten. I wonder, as he scoops up death with his dark flat shovel, if he looks for life, if he turns his head and bends so that his ear grazes each found garbage bag, and if he stops to weigh discarded parcels with his large worker hands. Does he sometimes tear open bags of litter dropped in arrogant thoughtlessness, just in case? I've never seen this man who works vampire hours, but I recall the strange reinterpretation of an American Gothic picture: man, upturned shovel, and pickup truck.

His services may not be needed so close to our woods. Our small road kill is always gone by morning. When a deer dies, we have to call the DNR, and the carcass may sit a few days. For our smaller corpses, foxes slip out of their dens under cover of night, spill down the curb like quiet dark shadows. And with their long sharp canines and incisors, they drag the unsightly dead out of sight and into the woods we were about to enter.

We found a trail after crossing a secondary stream. DJ jumped across, chiding me, "Come on. It's easy." I followed, showing him with my clumsy landing that I couldn't cross a stream even a hair wider than this one.

I windmilled my arms forward to pull my heels up from the soft bank and to prevent my seat from splatting in the muck. As soon as my feet were planted solidly under me, I swung my arms straight up and hyperextended my back in a gymnast pose. At my current weight, I must have looked like a Soviet shot-putter pretending to be gymnast Courtney Mc-Cool. McCool and I both have blonde ponytails.

DJ offered, "I give you a two point two," and pointed to our trail. He picked out deer tracks of different sizes, trying to count how many different deer had left their mark. A raccoon's front paw left an impression that resembled a small human hand with long, pointy nails. We shoved and jostled, competing for the lead spot on the trail, which was too narrow to allow us to walk abreast.

He loves to push and pull almost as much as he used to like to cuddle with me. His latest thing is to catch me standing near the bed, which he perceives as stunt mattress. He assumes his lineman position, runs, and tackles me, knocking me onto the bed. The same adolescence that's sprouting hair all over his body has lengthened him so that his aunt and grandmother look up to his face. Where there used to be baby fat, firm muscles now define his flesh. He's private about his body now. We have video of him, my last child, dashing down the hall naked and slapping his own butt. That playful freedom has been replaced with pride in his increasing strength. So, I played and let him knock into me and pull and push me on the trail.

I took a wide step in front of him, cutting him off with my leg, and ran ahead. Low to the ground, I spotted two triangles of reddish tan fur. Oh, ears, I thought, and a head. But the body flattened, so the whole thing looked like a red fox rug lying askew on the forest floor and assuming the entire width of the trail. For a second I was fascinated, but then repulsed by busy maggot eyes and black carrion beetles feverishly animating the fur with their group undulations. Flies formed a buzzing helmet-like force field around the death. I realized I hadn't breathed and couldn't inhale. I ran back on the trail; maneuvering around DJ, I said, "Euww, I don't want to be near it." I didn't want to smell the rotten pungency either. A few yards behind my son, I turned around.

DJ stepped toward the carcass, closer than I'd been, and he stood transfixed at the consummation of this body. "Dad and I found a deer in here last year, but it was just bones. It wasn't gross like this fox." He'd saved the deer skull in a shoebox. He'd taken it to school where the teacher allowed his classmates crowd around the cleaned-up death.

I'd acted like a girl, and he knew it was his job to be my antonym. He calmly walked back to join me in the place I'd found my breath. "Mom, how do you think he died?"

"Don't know, but foxes in the wild only live about five years. Usually, they crawl back into their dens to die." I told him what I knew, but not what he asked.

We pushed aside the thick brush beneath a canopy of maples and bur oak trees. The brush was replaced by sparse grass, and then the forest floor was cleared of all small vegetation. Light diminished where a few immense gnarled trees created a room with a ceiling of dense leaves and a floor of compact gray dirt with hundreds of underground roots surfacing just enough to create a shallow labyrinth that could only hint at the enormity of the tree-life below the soil. DJ touched the furrowed bark of the largest tree and asked what it was.

"Looks like a big old elm tree," I answered while searching the backpack for my *Trees of Wisconsin* guide. "I don't think it's an America elm. Most of those were wiped out by Dutch elm disease." I explained that I'd only heard of the elm-lined streets of the Midwest and Northeast that provided elegant shade to my grandparents' generation. While I babbled on and searched through the tree book, DJ interrupted me.

"Look down here." He nodded to a series of diminutive chalky batons scattered near the base of the tree, four bones from limbs and one rib. "Too big for a squirrel. Maybe a groundhog." We both bent down forming a silent huddle while we inspected the bones.

DJ spoke. "Everything dies."

Right here is the place where I'm supposed to have the answers, I thought. I should give him the wisdom that will offer comfort at my death and insight that he'll pass on to his children on a summer walk in decades to come.

As a nurse and daughter, I'd seen death. Two years earlier, my stepfather—the man I called "Pop"—died from prostate cancer. Anomalous cells grew in his body. The aberrant proliferation killed him, and only then, by their own rampant quest to take over his body, did the cancer itself die.

Pop lived at our home most of the last six weeks before his death. DJ had passed his report card over the bars of the hospital bed to him and played Christmas songs on his keyboard to cheer him up. Pop closed his eyes to listen and name the tunes:

"'O, Holy Night.' That's so beautiful.

'We Three Kings.' I haven't heard that in years.

'Silent Night.' That's tremendous, DJ, tremendous."

Like many cancer patients, Pop died in pieces: couldn't walk, couldn't stand, couldn't turn in bed, then nothing. In those last twenty-four hours, I'd given him a bed bath, and he moaned when I repositioned his gaunt body as gingerly as I knew how.

"Oh, Pop. I'm sorry."

"It's not you, it's me," he comforted me. "Just do what you need to do."

Later that day when I ran an errand to the store, Mom locked herself out of the house when she stepped outside to speak to a neighbor. She called me from the neighbor's house, crying as she explained that Pop was alone. I raced back, entered through the garage door, and rushed to check on Pop, who lay on a hospital bed in the living room.

"You okay, Pop?"

"Yes."

"Did you know you were alone? Mom locked herself out."

"Go let her in."

When I opened the front door, a December chill and my crying mother entered.

Pop strained to yell, "Did you find her?"

"Yes. She's fine."

"Thank you."

Pop died in his sleep that night, never losing the kindness and essence of who he was through the process. I gave a eulogy at Pop's funeral.

I didn't then—nor later in the presence of that great tree—have anything momentous to say about the meaning of death. I could only tell the truth of how his love for life seemed to grow and mingle with his impending death.

A few hundred yards away from the tree and old bones, in the space I'd run away from, carrion beetles feasted on maggots born in the flesh of the fox. The entire forest is a composition of bits of organic matter that come from life feeding on death. Remnants of foxes, tadpoles, wild geraniums, and trout lilies had perhaps cycled through the people who lived near this place. Liberace, Spencer Tracy, and Golda Meir had lived near our home. Perhaps some elements, molecules, and bits from their bodies had been reused in DJ's stiff brown hair. The body recycles its elements at different rates, but about every decade, each atom of a body that is a part of living tissue is new. Calcium from native Potawatomi Indians might have been reused in the bones that DJ poked at with his tattered basketball shoe.

Every element that passed out of my body in the form of my son is now in use elsewhere. He follows the patterns of his own DNA blended from his parents, but the organs, cells, and atoms have all formed anew from reclaimed oddments of life and death.

As soon as that fox died, *E. coli* and other organisms already present in its gut proliferated in the hypoxic and acidic environment. The gut burst and spread the feeding organisms to the rest of the corpse. Bacterial and fungal parents engendered hundreds of generations of offspring in a few days. Yellow jackets, flies, and earthworms shared the bounty of the life-giving putrefaction and began new families. Soil mites, nematodes, and nitrogen-fixing bacteria moved into the fox's rich neighborhood. As many as a trillion live cells reside in one cubic centimeter of soil near decomposing remains. "Everything dies," he'd said, but I hadn't responded and couldn't even determine if it was the life or death at the site of the dead fox that had repelled me.

All I'd discovered was that the tree wasn't an American elm. The living tree was an easier subject to discern. Its location near water and the reddish tint in the furrows of the rough bark revealed it as a slippery elm. By its size, I guessed it had been drinking from this river for over

100 years. Native Americans gave leaves of the slippery elm to the sick and dying to soothe their dry mouths. They treated boils and sores with poultices and ingested parts of the inner reddish bark to treat colitis and infection. An impressive tree. DJ had only asked its name but listened to my expanded explanation.

He started toward a deer trail, touching the trunks of trees with alternate hands, identifying the ones he knew: "Sugar maple, black willow, green ash, oak ..." Our trail led to the edge of the river, then to the point where we'd had to climb out of the low river bed to cross a bridge back in a neighborhood of houses, cars, and health walkers. A man in 1970-style running shorts walked in front of us smoking a cigarette. DJ quietly laughed at his shorts and his exposed long boiled-egg-white thighs bizarrely antithetical to the long, baggy shorts that were currently the style. The cigarette smoke reached up through my nose to my brain to pull open a file drawer and summon the face of a patient I cared for when I was a new nurse. I'd seen her face hundreds of times. Her hungry eyes searched for a comfort that came only when her breathing stopped. I told DJ about this first patient I ever cared for during a death—how she squeezed my hand, pinching my fingers into a tight bundle as she labored to breathe. Her family smoked in the waiting room, waiting for their matriarch to die of lung cancer. Despite high doses of intravenous analgesic and anti-anxiety medication, my patient struggled through her last breaths. Sitting erect, she reached for air as the cancer nicked off blood vessels and filled each of her alveoli with blood until there were no little air sacs left with a surface that could exchange carbon dioxide for oxygen. She drowned in her own blood as she clutched my hand. Seconds before I closed her wide-open eyes, an image of her face filed itself in my head. The smoky smell of the waiting room where I announced her death, labeled the file.

DJ recognized the anti-smoking agenda in my tale and diverted me with an invitation to play, asking why the guy would put on old running shorts to go out and smoke.

"Maybe thirty years ago he found love on this parkway. They were both betrothed to others but couldn't say goodbye. They promised to reunite here today wearing the same clothes so they would recognize each other."

DJ looked far ahead searching for the short-short wearer's beloved, but we only saw a wide man with bulldog legs and two white poodles. He shook his head. "Nah, I don't think so."

I wrinkled my nose and shook my head no.

DJ countered, "Maybe he's an alien from a planet that planned his disguise to fit in from watching reruns from the sports channel that show the old classic basketball games."

I saw a trail that led away from the sidewalk. "Yeah, that's probably it."

We let the matter drop, although sometimes we can banter until we have dozens of scenarios. Our path took us back into the undeveloped space along the river. A stand of prairie grass on a hill above the river was dotted with sweet pea vines and greeted us with a baby fresh scent so significant to their identity that their Latin name is *Lathyrus odoratus*, meaning, "fragrant pea." A soft breeze in seventy-five-degree air atomized the cologne. Daisy fleabane edged the prairie field. They beaconed pollinators with their bull's eye yellow centers and finely toothed petals that emerged from the capitulum as white. At exactly the halfway point of the petal, their color sharply changed to lavender, conferring the effect of a small target with a lovely color palette. The showy deep red bull thistles towered over the grasses.

DJ remembered, "Those are the spiny ones."

"Let's stand still for a minute and see if there are goldfinches around." Goldfinches line their nests with thistle down and eat the long, dark seeds—their favorite food. In less than a minute of stillness, we spotted five bright yellow males and four of the duller females scattered in the grasses and shrubs.

"Okay, you saw them. You see them in the yard every day. Now, can we move on?"

"Lead the way," I told him. I liked the idea that the finches came to visit our yard and feeders every day, and we finally paid an overdue call to their home. July brought our neighborhood a fresh heat that perfused life and death.

An expanse of mowed grasses between a lagoon and river let us walk abreast. DJ hung his elbow around my shoulder and leaned on me while we walked. I tilted in, trying to make it easy for him to maintain the position that crinkled my neck.

We walked silently until DJ blurted, "I believe in heaven and, and I think—I hope—we get to live forever."

This was my second opportunity to say something deep. "Jesus is our Savior, and because we believe in Him we do have everlasting life."

He huffed. My response—too scripted for him. My neck hurt where the crook of his elbow tugged. He said nothing.

I grew quiet. Thoughts of death lead to God because we must find a way to make peace with the end of life. The minister and writer F. Forrester Church said, "Religion is the human response to being alive and having to die." I'd been exploring Unitarianism and was attracted to the faith's searching for spiritual truths in Christianity, Judaism, nature, and Eastern religions. I hadn't decided if my worshiping with Unitarians was an insult to my religious roots or a bridge between Christianity and openness to a spirituality not tied to dogma. The search felt right, even without a conclusion.

A large gray-blue S caught my eye in the lagoon. We stopped and turned while DJ kept his arm hooked around my neck. The bed of the lagoon heaved with pollywogs and crayfish. A great blue heron stalked: stab, toss, catch, swallow. A graceful maneuver carried out with such adeptness, we waited only a few minutes to see a replay of this death feeding life, judged beautiful.

On the way home, we stopped at the Burleigh Street Bridge, where five willows along the east side of the river reached for their own apparition. The largest tree tilted its trunk to reach across four white boulders and wept into its own specter and having touched it, had to strain to stay erect as the reflection slowly pulled the willow into the river. A quarter-mile upstream an old willow lay uprooted, stripped, and bleached across the moving water.

We shared the bridge with the automobile traffic behind us. In front of us and above the river, barn swallows with their red bellies, forked tails, and blue bodies flashed iridescent in the sun as they flew. They swooped and caught insects to feed the giant open beaks of the babies who sat in tidy cups under the bridge. We knew they would soon fledge and keep pace with their parents, who fly up to six hundred miles a day in the swift seasonal winds. The offspring will learn to feed themselves and to fly to Argentina and back, and then they will not need their parents anymore.

The river ran beneath our feet, the water constantly wandered through our lives, atmosphere, and our bodies. Even my thoughts about this river were connected to others who watched the water move through their own years. Leonardo da Vinci said, "In rivers, the water that you touch is the last of what has passed and the first of that which comes; so with present time." Two hydrogen atoms join one oxygen atom to create a molecule that is slightly positive at one of the poles and slightly negative on the other. The positive end of one pole weakly attracts the negative pole of another water molecule in an act called polar bonding. A small electric charge gives the water surface tension and the ability to dissolve more substances than any other solvent. Water moves up tree trunks and through veins and rivers. It carries life through time. Those hydrogen and oxygen atoms formed molecules that have been flowing through lives since the beginning of the existence of life on this planet, and not just the elements of water, but this water—the water that moved beneath the willows and bridge and this mother and son. DJ stared out into the river and spoke, "Mom, I do believe in God and life after death. I just don't know what that life will be."

"That's what faith is—when you don't understand exactly but believe anyway."

"Yeah. It'll drive you nuts if you think you've got to figure it all out, but you still have to think about it some. I don't know if Grandpa Paul went away to heaven. Sometimes I think I feel him with us."

"Do you feel him now?" I asked.

DJ's pensive profile showed eyebrows bushier than I remembered. His nose had grown out of the pug stage that mine never left. "The woods felt so busy today, like we were not alone."

"I felt it too," I said. It was like all of our ancestors and all those who lived before us came for a July reunion.

When John Muir was ten, a year younger than DJ, he came to live in the wilderness of Wisconsin. Near here, he began his journey to become a wilderness theologian. Years later, he gave parents this advice:

> "Let the children walk with Nature, let them see the beautiful blendings and communions of death and life, their joyous inseparable unity, as taught in woods and meadows, plains and mountains and streams of our blended star, and they will learn that death is stingless indeed, and as beautiful as life."

My faith isn't that strong. Death can be stingless, but it doesn't always show up as a natural phenomenon of intellectual and spiritual beauty. Having no choice, I make a conditional peace with death but can't quite commit to a universal embrace of the face of mortality. I've seen death many times; I've been in the room. I can't shake this fallacious belief that everyone is owed a long life. I'm angry about terrorists and politicians who kill to demonstrate their power, and I won't find a way to think of murder and genocide as beautiful. Why are we unable to prevent that kind of pain and suffering? I hope there is not a divine plan that is meant to create a Danteesque tension between life and death. No one need drop a bomb on a village so that I might appreciate the quality and quantity of my life by comparison.

I can buy Muir's explanation when the dead and dying are decades older than I am and die a natural death. The idea of life as a cycle, the reuse, the rebirth, and the constant freshness of new life mixed with the seasoned, I see the beauty and sense in this. Maybe DJ will make a more complete peace with the reality of death than I've been able to.

DJ stared at the river. He wasn't looking at me; he wasn't looking to me. "Everything dies," DJ had told me. It wasn't a question; it was an acknowledgement.

The phone rang as I put the key in the door lock. DJ ran around me, making a show of speed-wiping his feet on the rug before his successful dash to the phone. He turned his back to me as a signal that the call was for him. I was washing my hands in the bathroom when I heard him yell to the whole house, "Mom, can Michael sleep over?" His voice cracked upward two scattered octaves in the middle of Michael's name.

Thank you God, for my son. I turned my head around for a moment to yell toward him, "Sure," and then smiled at myself in the mirror, pleased in the way that parents delight in the intelligence and innocence of their offspring. I love to watch DJ pursue answers and think about big questions. Pascal, who devoted his life to science and religion, said about God, "You would not seek me had you not found me."

My face was flushed, and my curly hair puffed out despite the rubber band holding it back. A black spot fluttered in my tangles—a flying ant. I carefully plucked it out and went to the front porch to release the hitchhiker. The neighbor's kid drove by in her new used car, at least fifteen miles over the speed limit. She waved to me with a teenage look-at-me-I'm-driving smile. The tall Queen Anne's lace flowers on the side of the road quivered as if they were an excited crowd, celebrating her privilege of passage.

Since before the seventh century, Buddhists have celebrated the July communion of the ancestors' visitation to the living. The origin of this sacred celebration is a mother and son story. While meditating, Mongallana saw his mother suffering in hell and pleaded to Buddha for her release. Buddha explained that the mother was cast to hell for her worldly ways, her most egregious act the placement of her family (especially her children) before all else—even her own spiritual development. Buddha advised this son that through meditation and the practice of compassionate acts and offerings, he could release his mother. Mongallana freed his mother from torment and in his joy danced the Bon, a dance that still surrounds the celebration of the reunion of spirits.

DJ came out on the porch with me and looked at the nothing-happening-on-the-parkway where I stared. He's accustomed to my silent focus on birds, trees, water, bugs, and flowers. "Michael will be here at four." He turned to go back into the house, but first mentioned, "Seems like there's more of them than last year."

"More of what?"

"More of those white flowers—the ones that start out looking like ferns and then turn lacy this time of year. I can tell you like them."

The door shut behind him. A yellow swallowtail butterfly explored the screen.

I've read that some modern Buddhists no longer believe that the spirits of the dead come back in July. New Agers changed the essence of the holiday to a time to honor the dead, and, of course, we should honor the departed. Still, I think ancestors are drawn to visit the living when called, if not throughout the year, certainly in July.

COUNTY OF ORIGIN

*"A community is the mental and spiritual condition of knowing
that the place is shared, and that the people who share the place
define and limit the possibilities of each other's lives."*
WENDELL BERRY

I said the names of those up-north towns as my mother had in the years of hula hoops, eight-track tape players, and unfettered sleeping in the back of our faux-wood station wagon. When we drove US Highway 141 north out of Green Bay to visit family, my mom always said the last hour of the trip passed quickest as we drove the two-lane highway through the Marinette County towns while she recited, as if recalling a well-loved poem, "Coleman, Pound, Beaver, Middle Inlet, Crivitz, Wausaukee, Amberg, Beecher, Pembine, Niagara." As a child, I'd thought she had us recite the list when we entered each town so we wouldn't ask any are-we-almost-there questions. Some of these hamlets were so small that by the time we completed the list, we'd passed the tavern, gas station, and church that anchored the settlement to the road, and we again bisected forests and farms.

Decades later, my son sat beside me on our way to the north woods that had never been my home but had always been where I came from. I'd grown up in Milwaukee, but my grandparents, aunts, uncles, and cousins lived near Wisconsin's border with upper Michigan. Any sense of having an extended family and immigrant homeland I ever felt touched me when we traveled to the land of forests and to our relatives. I wanted DJ to feel a connection to these people who still lived in the rural setting of our English and German ancestors. I wanted him to love the land and the people that I loved. Because we visited only once or twice a year, I didn't know if it were possible for him to develop a visceral connection to his rural and agricultural heritage. His older and grown sister, Andrea, missed the connection because I was caught up in graduate school and full-time work and missed several years of family gatherings. The end of her childhood caught me by surprise.

DJ and I were not traveling on US 141 because we drove in from a Boulder Junction Scout Camp, but my voice repeated the sequence of towns as if the recitation were a requirement to cross into Marinette County. I'd engineered a way to meet all family obligations and to fit in a nature outing as well: Thursday with Mom and her new husband at their Mole Lake cabin, a Friday trip to Boulder Junction to pick up DJ from Scout Camp, a Saturday family reunion at Morgan Park, and on Sunday, DJ and I would have our hikes to a few Marinette waterfalls. By Monday, we'd be back to our Milwaukee suburb in time for DJ to begin football practice.

I thought I'd never seen any of the falls in the county that calls itself the "Waterfalls Capital of Wisconsin," but my reunion relatives told me I had seen them as a child. "You'll remember Long Slide when you see it." Aunt Lil referred to her dad, my Grandpa Ed. "Daddy used to fish for trout on the Pemebonwon River right below the falls; he probably took you."

Cousin Susie recommended Dave's Falls, just south of Amberg, because a lady at the bank had her wedding pictures taken there. Uncle Kenny overheard our conversation and lumbered over to us, swinging his cane and leaning his body from side to side as he raised each of his bowed bulldog legs. He suggested if we were going to Long Slide and Dave's Falls, we might as well hit Smalley Falls because it was between the other two. In the morning, DJ and I left the map in the glove box and followed the family directions to our first destination by turning at the big white boulder across from the tamarack swamp.

The Long Slide Falls sign warned "Dangerous Overlook" as we entered a parking lot of sparse gravel and grasses. We scanned the perimeter of the lot and didn't see a trail but heard the muffled tumult of falling water behind a forest that bulged over the edges of the clearing and obscured any openings into the woods.

By searching the soil in the direction of the distant clamor, we found a tan stripe in the edge of the woodland floor that served as the trail to the falls. I pushed away a cedar branch and looked back at my son who reached forward to hold the bough doorway open. His hand was in sync to push back the limb so we could have continued in a seamless stride through the obstruction. Instead, I stopped, turned, and looked at his sun-bronzed face. I'd kissed and hugged him when he appeared as soon as I stepped out of the van at the Scout campground, but I'd been so busy with reunion shopping, cooking, and catching up with the relatives that I hadn't looked at him. We hadn't talked much because he'd been eager to listen to his iPod—a forbidden electronic device at Scout camp. He liked camp but hadn't told me much more than that.

"What?" he asked, wondering why I wasn't moving.

We stood holding the arm of the same tree at a welcoming threshold amidst the fresh scent of cedar. "Thanks for coming with me. I always wanted to see the waterfalls."

"It's okay. I like this stuff too."

I realized there were no people around, and the faint hint of trail suggested there hadn't been many here all summer. This was bear country, and we'd both seen a huge black bear cross the Kremlin Road near here last year. And only a few days previously, on my way to visit my mom, I'd missed a turn and pulled to the side of the road to check my map near a stand of brown-eyed Susans and high bush cranberries. I had been driving Route 29, which runs atop a drumlin, a ridge left by a glacier. Across the road, a wetland hosted families of redhead ducks that flew en masse in a disorganized V as I pulled over. Beyond a meadow, the landscape displayed hardwood forests, stands of Jack pines, a few tidy farms with domed silos, chaste red barns, and fields that hugged the curves of glaciated land as if an artist had brushed tractor strokes over an earthen canvas.

I tried to reorient myself to developing a driving plan, but the soprano notes of a shy bird (whose carbonated "Bob-o-link" song named him) pulled my attention out of the map toward the roadside meadow. I simultaneously smelled what I first thought was the odor of wet grasses wafting in from the marsh. The scent intensified, and I felt a heavy darkness rambling toward me from across the road. He must have been 600 pounds of black bear—the biggest I'd ever seen, and I lived three years in Alaska. Females only grow to a maximum of 400 pounds, so I knew this was a male swinging his head in time to the movements of his limbs. The yellow knife-blades of his claws ticked the blacktop. His nostrils flared and explored different directions. I fumbled for my window switches and got my driver's side one up right away and then forgot how to push the button for the passenger window. It pulsated up and down a few frantic times before I was sealed in glass and metal. My car wasn't a safe zone; he could smash the window if he wanted to. The engine was running, so I shifted the car into drive but kept my foot on the brake. The bear looked at me briefly— not at the van, but directly at me—before he swung his head to create a little more momentum to change his trajectory and cross behind me. The reality that this was his dominion overtook me. I was afraid and drove off in a westward direction away from the bear, forgetting all about my urge to reference a map. In my rearview mirror, I saw the upward thrust of a big black rump as the behemoth bounded into the brush, and my fear changed to excitement that I had seen the bear up close.

Shadows of imagined bears had been stalking me since that encounter, and as we entered the quiet woods, I imagined the possibility of these dark menaces beyond each turn in the path. I looked over my shoulder and started to talk loudly to DJ, who followed me on the thin trail to the falls. "DID YOU SWIM MUCH AT CAMP?"

"YES. I PASSED THE CLASS A SWIM TEST. WHY ARE WE YELLING?"

"I FORGOT THE BEAR WHISTLE."

"LET'S CLAP INSTEAD."

He reminded me that bears generally sleep during the day, and I reminded him that sometimes they don't. We stopped shouting and clapped occasionally as we walked toward the sound of rushing water. Our noisy intrusion into the woods meant we would scare away most of the wildlife, which seemed like a good plan, safety meriting priority over interaction with the fauna.

I applauded DJ as he descended a steep, rocky part of the trail ahead of me. A mature basswood tree with heart-shaped leaves stood in the center of the drop and gave him a place to halt his downward momentum before he continued on. When I started down, my acceleration made me hit the tree with enough force to inspire an arboreal embrace with the one-foot diameter trunk. When I reached around and hugged the tree in a restful pose, DJ laughed at me for looking like I was making-out with the pillar. Gravity, like a magnet, kept me attracted as I turned my head and pressed my cheek to the softly textured bark. The embrace felt mutual, and I imagined that the basswood enjoyed my familiarity. I patted the tree, pushed myself up and around its support, and tested the rocky descent with the toes of my sneakers on the way to catch up with my son. When I reached DJ, I wanted to tell him more about my basswood make-out buddy. Pointing back at the tree, I was surprised that I imagined a fleshy hook in place of my hand.

Grandpa Ed, who knew the forest as if he had created it, had lost several fingers in a saw accident as a young man. His index finger and half of his middle finger curved out of the paddle of his palm in a stiff contracture. A single yellowed and pointed nail served as the sharpened point of his clawed hand. He'd pointed at trees in this forest and told me the names and what I believed to be all there was to know about these woods. Even though I carry guidebooks and look up facts and histories, I credit Grandpa Ed for each scrap of forest knowledge I possess.

That basswood, also called a linden, gave me a benevolent feeling, and I felt camaraderie with John Muir. When he felt close to a tree, he'd call it one of his "tree people," and refer to its humanity. Possibly, it was a conceited human act to personify the helpful nature of the tree, but we don't have an unbiased language for friendships across species. In June and July, bracts of the basswood's hanging cream flowers offer the forest its sweet summer smell and nectar for honeybees. When the blossoms have been fertilized and the bloom withers, fruit emerges in the form of small nutlets to sustain the birds. The tree is sometimes called bastwood, because bast, lashings, can be woven from strips of its fibrous inner bark.

When amputees walked on wooden legs, they walked because of this strong and lightweight wood that is still used for, among other things, toys and musical instruments. Native Americans made syrup from the sap and bandages from the bark. They ate the young leaves and boiled the cambium for tea and soup. Basswood settles for only 25 percent sunlight and adapts to sparse soil on rocky ledges. It doesn't ask for much. Even in old age and death, it continues its service by decaying quickly and opening its pulpy body as a shelter for woodland birds and animals.

DJ and I stuck our heads out of a small opening we created when we parted a curtain of green branches. But we could only see a slice of the waterfall, too small a picture to be able to appreciate the scope of the long slide of falling water. Doubling back to an alternate trail, we found a rocky ledge substantial enough to create a viewing platform.

The water didn't drop over a ledge; it didn't spill over rocks. This water pummeled boulders the size of houses and arched around outcroppings and vertical juttings and frothed in solid white permanence. DJ looked at ahead of us at a green-gray canyon-like wall that angled fifty-feet of waterfall toward us.

"These rocks are tough looking. What are they?"

"Know those bluffs in the town of Niagara, the ones right before you cross into Iron Mountain?"

"Yeah."

"These are part of the same geologic formation, the Niagara Escarpment." Dolomite, calcium, and magnesium carbonate forged from pressurized skeletons and seashells that lived on a subtropical reef more than 400 million years ago during the Silurian period formed these ledges. Volcanic movements mauled and mixed this sturdy rock that was tinted blue in spots by igneous ash and covered by millions of years of sediment and veined by granite. Billions of tons of ice shoved, scratched, gouged, upwarped, and exposed the ledge during five different glacial ages. This was some tough old rock.

Imagining this rock as originating from a living coral reef and other skeletal remains made us both think about the stony shelf that supported us. This rock came from animal life. DJ reminded me that in science class they'd taught him to determine if objects were animal, vegetable, or mineral, but he questioned the classifications. If animals were in minerals, minerals were in animals, and vegetables were in animals (hadn't I made him eat salad last night?) they are not really separate. Weren't they all connected? In the essay, "Nature," Emerson, like DJ, considered the unity of nature. "So intimate is this Unity, that it is easily seen, it lies under the undermost garment of nature, and betrays its source in Universal Spirit."

DJ's finger traced one of several long glacial fissures scoring the rock ledge that supported us. "Does the town of Niagara have anything to do with Niagara Falls?"

"Yes. It's all the Niagara Escarpment. The ledge sits over Lakes Michigan and Huron like a baseball cap. The tip of the bill is Niagara Falls."

As we hiked back to the car, DJ said this would be a good place to film a dinosaur movie and proposed a scene where a *Spinosaurus egypticus* would tear into a stegosaur at the top of the Long Slide and the camera could follow the immense guts and organs as they violently somersault down the bloody falls.

"Lovely."

Back on the Kremlin Road loop, we talked about my grandma's and grandpa's old farm site on this road. DJ never knew them or the farm. My mom and her six older siblings grew up without an indoor bathroom. The only running water was a pump in the kitchen sink. My aunts called the pump a luxury because they remembered when the well was outside and would freeze up in the winter. All that's left of the farm site now is a pile of dark gray boards from one of the barns. They are barely visible in the tall, almond-colored grasses and lay as if the fallen barn was on its last slow-motion bounce before settling into death.

As children, my older sister Julie and I had visited this farm. I remembered one night when she wouldn't go with me to the outhouse because I'd refused to go with her when she'd asked me hours before. I sat in the outhouse in a pink, polka-dot nightgown, my flashlight trembling into the black night, while I sang to scare the bears away. I sat on the hole dangling my mukluk slippers and belted out "I'm a Little Teapot." When I got to the "…tip me over and pour me out" part, I leaned and shone the light into the upper corners of the wooden privy house revealing a spider's nest with multiple large trapped packages. Every verse got louder, and I was screaming about being a little teapot on the way back into the house until I closed the door into the farmhouse and silently tiptoed back to bed. We'd pumped water in the kitchen and heated it on the stove to wash dishes, playing Little House on the Prairie. We swept mice "seeds" from the corners where Grandma Bertha couldn't see them. Julie and I dared each other to penetrate the swaybacked rotting barn. The creaking and straining floorboards warned us not to go in too far, but we would enter individually and sidestep to the left where the floor was silent. Light shone through chinks in the walls, designing angular stripes in the dust and spider webs of midair. Our mom remembered only shreds of red on what had been a cowshed years before her memory could make lasting imprints; that barn was always old. And because my mother was the youngest of seven, my grandparents, too, were always old to me. They were not beautiful people, though Grandma's hair remained naturally dark black into her seventies, and her cotton stockings covered shapely calves that we'd seen only when we'd glimpsed her starting up the woodstove before she dressed for the day. Beneath the hem of her housedress and above the ties of her beige oxfords, she showed thick cotton stockings in shades of beige. Sometimes they didn't match. Grandpa didn't like to wear his false teeth, and his idea of combing the white hair on the sides of his bald head was to push the wayward strands back and away from his face.

DJ listened to my reminiscence and shook a little with silent laughter, repeating "I'm a little teapot," as we turned one driveway past where the lightning had split a white pine tree last spring.

I didn't leave the car once we'd parked but continued telling DJ about the great grandparents he never met. If you'd seen Grandpa on the street in town, it would have been easy to assume that the pot-bellied man with a long-underwear shirt and suspenders was an uneducated hick. He never went to college, but he could repair an engine without a manual and with parts pulled from junked vehicles left in the woods; he could build a shed and calculate the board-foot requirements of lumber and shingles without ever putting a pencil to paper. It would be easy for more cultured people to feel superior to him when discussing nuances of French wine or operatic translations, but if they put on their hiking boots and came to his territory, they would be daunted by his complex understanding of the lands of the north woods. And they would be humbled by Grandma's generosity, because once she knew any visitor's favorite baked good, she'd plan to place the warm treat as a centerpiece on the aluminum-edged table as they crossed the threshold of her kitchen. Sometimes Grandma and Grandpa gave off a rank odor: Grandpa like the musty basement, Grandma like rose water and compost. And Grandpa always dominated the family as if his authoritarian stewardship was essential to survival. But their lives were based on their understanding of doing the next right thing, never on acquisition or self-indulgence. As I opened the car door to continue our walk, I told DJ that I still missed my grandparents.

Smalley Falls met us with a warning sign depicting a toddler on a mountain with a line drawn diagonally across the unwanted child. Hemlock, sugar maple, and yellow birch surrounded the blunted road that served as a parking lot. We clapped again, and DJ asked me condescendingly if I'd be "Okay on the steep trail?"

"If I have trouble, you can carry me."

DJ snorted at this impossibility and began the hike. On one of the descents, he raised his arms and jumped to the bottom and then looked up at me in did-you-see-that confidence. I applauded for the last time, as DJ then found two solid sticks to bang together for the rest of the hike.

A rock jutted out over the smallish falls after the steepest section of the descent. The water rushed down a rocky S-curve and continued on in a series of white water rapids nearly as far as our vision could discern before the Pemebonwon turned left and departed from view. I told DJ the scenery looked familiar. "I think I was here with Grandpa Ed on a cold, early spring day. He caught some trout and showed me a dark cylinder about ten inches long; he called it a 'bear plug.' Said it was a kind of scat that forms inside a bear's rectum during hibernation. They pass the hard stopper when they awake and start eating again."

"Ah, yes, that first poop of spring," DJ kidded. "Why do you think they don't want kids here?"

"Small kids are unpredictable, and this is not a place to be careless."

"Know what the worst thing about camp was?" DJ asked. He told me about how some of the Scouts just wouldn't do dishes and were not careful about littering, and he noticed how other kids had to clean up after them. He said he noticed that at our family reunion, no one had to be told not to litter or to help clean up, and there were lots of children there.

When the party had wound down, the kids scanned the cabin and surrounding land and found only a rusty 7-Up can. The aunts and Mom heated dishwater in the kitchen of the cabin we'd rented for the reunion. We had a stove, but the water pump was outside. Those of us old enough to remember talked about washing dishes with Grandma Bertha when her eyesight was poor. She insisted on washing, and she'd leave so much food on the dishes that we'd have to sneak them back to the dirty pile. Grandma complained, "Will these dishes never end?" but she never seemed to figure it out.

If we tried the direct approach, "Grandma, there's still a little spot on this one," she always had the same answer, and all the aunties and cousins in the kitchen repeated Grandma's lesson in unison: "It's a poor dish dryer who can't wipe off a little dirt."

When Aunt Alice's dishwashing skills were found lacking, Aunt Evie made an exaggerated nonchalant show of putting the au-gratin potato spoon back in the dirty pile. By the time we got to the difficult pans that needed scrubbing, we shared stories and cried about Cousin Peggy, who died in a car accident only five days after last year's reunion. While Aunt Evie cried about her daughter's death, she kept washing dishes and telling stories about how beautifully Peggy had decorated her new house and how Peggy could stack a cord of wood in a perfect wall that would never fall no matter how swift the wind blew or how much snow would weigh down the stack. The last time DJ and I had seen Peggy was the day after the last reunion in her new dream house that she and her husband, Jerry, had built for their impending retirement years. She'd moved back to Marinette County near Niagara, family, and the land she'd grown up on. She and Jerry had planned to retire, but the stock market plunge after September 11 had taken too much of their savings. "We were lucky," she'd told me, "because I found a bookkeeping job nearby at the Home Depot in Iron

Mountain." She never got to retire and never found a reason to complain.

I remembered Cousin Angie's girls at the campfire one night before in their grass-stained pastel shorts sitting on dirt and dry grass because there were not enough chairs for everyone. DJ had offered his seat, but the girls refused. We were the out-of-town relatives, and the up-north code of hospitality granted us special consideration. The heat of the fire, the cool night, and the ashy coating on their incinerated marshmallows did not bother these freckled eight- and nine-year-old beauties. No one in this family expected to be pampered or believed that comfort was a natural state.

Uncle Bill was seventy-eight and still built stone fireplaces and chimneys, but he explained that he liked Auntie Lil or a lady to decide what colors looked best together. He shouted in the hard-of-hearing voice that DJ liked to mimic, "WHAT IN THE HELL DO I KNOW ABOUT COLOR COORDINATION?"

We kept talking about the family as we turned away from the sounds of the thundering falls. Aunt Evie, who's close to eighty, rides her bike to the neighbors. She fishes whenever she can, which has been not been often lately because her husband, Uncle Claude, has been in a leg cast all summer. Auntie describes his cast as running "from his ankle to two inches from you-know-where." Aunt Alice, now a widow, visited Costa Rica, Wyoming, and California since last year's reunion. She was looking forward to getting some more miles on the snow machine she bought last year when she turned seventy. As we entered the car, I told DJ he could look in the gift box in the back seat to see the present Cousin Cheri, Peggy's only sister, gave me—a primitive carving of two sitting women sharing conversation. Cheri and I each had only one sibling, a sister. She wanted me to appreciate what I still had, even if my Julie did live far away in Alaska. Cheri wasn't bitter about what she'd lost but had said she was lonely.

The Kremlin road met 141, and we turned south toward Pembine. I turned into the eight-block residential district to show DJ the gray-shingled house that Grandma and Grandpa moved to when they sold the farm. He thought the house with its gravelly white trim and brown lawn looked dumpy, and it did. But the indoor plumbing, bathtub, and hot water—right from the tap—and at least two electric outlets in every room had been an exciting luxury for the couple back in the sixties.

On the way to our last falls, I recited, "After Pembine comes Beecher, then Amberg." Just south of Amberg, we turned into the manicured county park built around Dave's Falls. DJ identified a tall plant with a club of yellow flowers on the edge of the large parking lot we shared with a dozen other vehicles. I'd taught him about the mullein and its practical use when having to go to the bathroom in the woods. He happily spotted them everywhere, calling them the "butt-wipe plant." I pretended irritation, but I didn't fool him.

Cleared marked trails, handicapped access, and a managed forest defined this park, groomed for beauty and human use. Even with a thirty-square-foot clearing for outhouses and wide trails where two or three could walk abreast, the canopy of forest offered dappled shade to every summer visitor. Birch, white pine, aspen, red pine, and sugar maple trees loosely filled the forest on each side of us. The faint sound of laughter and rushing water met our ears just as we saw the Pike River make a wide turn. A hardwood bridge lightly arched over the river, and another trail turned upstream. We crossed to the middle of the bridge and faced the falls. It was easy to imagine this setting decorating mantles and hanging walls all over the county as a background in smiling portraits of wedding couples. Frothy rapids preceded the fifteen-foot falls. Ledges of quartz and granite flanked the chute and sparkled in the sunlight. Three couples played, jumping from the ledges and falling parallel to the plunging water.

The attenuated forest allowed the wind to sift through and skim scents from cedar, hardwoods, and the river. DJ spotted a white pine about fifty feet high and wondered if that might have been a survivor from before the loggers deforested most of Wisconsin.

White pine brought loggers to these woods in the mid-1800s, when some of the pines were 150 feet tall, three feet across, and over 400 years old. Two or three trees could build a good-sized house. Most of Chicago was built with Wisconsin white pine. Thoreau visited Wisconsin in 1861 and admired the sturdy spires here, as he did in Maine, once writing that, "Every creature is better alive than dead, men and moors and pine trees. It is the living spirit of tree, not its spirit of turpentine, with which I sympathize and which heals my cut. It is as immortal as I am, and perchance will go to as high a heaven, there to tower above me still."

Thoreau was an exception, because most people of that time saw the giant white pine as a resource to be exploited. By the 1930s, only five percent of the original woodlands survived in Marinette County. It wasn't until nearly all of the trees were gone that the people of the county started setting aside forests both for conservation and for management of timberlands.

DJ and I walked to the river, took off our shoes, and stood in a calm, sandy pool across from the playful couples. We both made lemon faces and stiffened our backs when our feet entered the cold river.

Over 125 years ago, when loggers felled the pines, the Boom Company used the Pike River to float the winter harvest to the Menomonee River and then to the sawmills in the city of Marinette. They clear-cut the land, taking all the trees and leaving piles of drying and flammable branches behind. The roaring water at these falls was often the site of life-threatening logjams. Lumberjacks who walked out to dislodge the mass risked being tossed into the violent waters and crushed between groaning timbers. Local stories continue about how Dave Frechette died clearing a jam at the then-named Pem-a-wan Falls in about 1881. Old timers used to tell stories about Dave's bravery and about his confident swagger across many jams before those last logs crushed him and rolled him under.

Grandpa Ed, born in 1892, had said that when he worked for a lumber company, he heard stories about loggers like Dave (good friends called him "Sandy") and heard more stories that went even further back to 1871 and the most disastrous fire in US history. Some of the older loggers and mill workers had lived through the Peshtigo Fire in eastern Marinette County. Grandpa had seen the scarred arms they'd used to splash Peshtigo River water over their heads in defense against the firestorm raging across the land and water.

Even though the Peshtigo Fire killed at least five times as many people as the Chicago fire, most don't know about the October 8 fire because Chicago burned on the exact same day. The city of Chicago, with its higher profile, overshadowed coverage of the fierce Wisconsin fire. A cyclonic fire whirl obliterated Peshtigo, killing about 900 city residents. The fire ran the entire length of the county and south, almost to the city of Green Bay and west across to parts of Brown, Kewaunee, and Door Counties. The flames wiped out twenty-three Wisconsin towns and took anywhere from 1,500 to 2,500 lives. Many bodies in Peshtigo were turned to cinder ashes, making it difficult to count corpses. A mass grave near the present-day Fire Museum holds at least 350 bodies. I'd visited the museum and cemetery once to see the graves of distant relatives. As difficult as it was to face the mass grave, a headstone and story of three children touched me enough to stand in a sudden Peshtigo downpour in frozen grief. That gravestone listed the names of "George, age one, and Ella, age four. Children of J.L. & A.M. Mellen. Perished in Peshtigo Fire, Oct. 8, 1871."

Their nineteen-year-old brother had carried them through burning streets to the Peshtigo River, where fireballs rolled across the water, but also where survival was possible. He held his baby brother and baby sister, one in each arm, for four hours, dunking and splashing them to prevent their consumption until finally the fiery tornado completed its destruction. He climbed out of the river clutching his charges, only to find they had both died of hypothermia.

The dry autumn had contributed to the fire, but clear-cut forests, piles of discarded tinder and sawdust, corduroy roads, and the careless burning practices of farmers had all acted as accelerants. Even after Peshtigo was rebuilt, the clear-cut logging practices in northern Wisconsin didn't peak until the 1890s. DJ thought that he had never heard the story of the Peshtigo Fire. Then, he remembered that Aunt Julie owned a rocking chair that he was not allowed to sit in because, although it had survived the fire, it was scarred by a charred runner.

As we sat to put on our shoes, DJ asked, "So, Grandpa Ed was a logger?"

I'd never thought of my tree-loving grandpa as a lumberjack, which was silly, because he lost his fingers in a lumber mill saw. "I guess he was."

After his accident, he became a farmer and a surveyor. He could point to a vista of trees and remember when the land was still dotted with charred stumps and when the CCC (Civilian Conservation Corps) replanted forests in fields that were clear cut and on farmlands after the owners wore out the land and left their barren acreage with log barns for grave markers.

Grandpa Ed was born in forest country, just about at the peak of deforestation. He'd seen this land at its worst, and he'd witnessed its slow return to woodland. For the first time I considered that our family's love of the land and woods and our desire not to screw it up flowed not only from a heritage of appreciation, but also from Grandpa's eye-witness experience of the molestation of this land. Perhaps those early settlers, who didn't feel a connection to the forest and who were struggling for survival, didn't have a vision of their destruction. Maybe they felt the forest gave its gift to build our homes and cities as an act of friendship.

Back on the road, we passed the city of Crivitz and crossed the Peshtigo River. DJ pecked at the details of the days, asking me more about Grandma Bertha's wood stove and the Uncle Cy he never met, who was a descendent of a Peshtigo Fire survivor. He asked about moose and elk. "Did they ever live in Wisconsin?"

I told him about how the deforested land had favored the white-tailed deer and about Aunt Lil's first husband, Uncle Cy, who died of cancer twenty-five years ago. I tried to explain how a wood-stove required an understanding how each species of wood burned to regulate the cooking temperature. It's difficult to bake a cake with birch logs; they burn too fast. The hot coals of hardwood work the best.

DJ looked out the window when we passed through Beaver Township. "This is where your Cousin Peggy had her accident, isn't it?"

I said, "Yes. She died near here," but in truth, we drove exactly over the spot of the fatal collision that snapped her neck.

DJ had been with Peggy, my sister Julie, and me on a walk less than a week before my cousin died. She showed us the variety of ferns growing along the Menomonee River and where the lady slippers bloomed in spring. We'd sat on logs she'd rolled from the forest to create a place to be still and listen. And when we sat quietly in the infancy of evening, the whip-poor-wills and warblers sang and delivered the concert just as Peggy had planned. When we heard the woods grow mute, the shrill cry of a hawk broke the silence.

Peggy planned her dream home for decades with Jerry, whom she'd loved since their days at Niagara High School. They'd saved for their land, raised two sons, and walked the ridge where they planned to build. They'd framed the view from the imagined windows with their hands and then measured out the rooms with their paces years before they hired an architect. From the windows of her realized dream, she'd pointed to the place the deer cross with their speckled fawns in the morning mist. Her finger swept the landscape to the place where she'd picked the blueberries we'd eaten in the morning pancakes. She was a part of her land.

African Conservationist Baba Dioum said, "In the end, we will conserve only what we love; we will love only what we understand; and we will understand only what we have been taught."

Before we left the reunion, Aunt Lil was already planning ahead. "Next year, I want all the grown cousins to have a night together. I'll host a Friday night campfire so the cousins can spend time together." The grandparents are gone. Uncle Lee died in World War II, and Uncle George died fifty-three years later in his Florida retirement home. Five siblings are left who grew up in the farmhouse. Seven cousins remain who pumped water at the kitchen sink, walked in the woods with Grandpa Ed, and cooked big farm breakfasts with Grandma Bertha. Behind Aunt Lil's plan for a session of cousin bonding was an acknowledgement that the oldest generation was likely to be the next to go, leaving the cousins to honor and pass on the family stories and traditions. I couldn't imagine a generation of second and third cousins (already geographically spreading across the country) meeting to remember the origins of great-great-great grandparents. Eventually, the reunions will end. The connective cord will snap. I wanted to believe that the place would always be there: the clear rushing waters, the forests, the bears, and the people who inhabit the land I came from.

Before we crossed the Marinette County line, I ran my list. "Niagara, Pembine, Beecher, Amberg, Wausaukee, Middle Inlet, Crivitz, Beaver, Pound, Coleman." DJ sat with his iPod ready in his lap. His lips moved with my recitation, and I saw them forming the words "Pound, Coleman." He waited until we crossed from Marinette to Oconto County before he stretched the earphones across his head.

SHEPHERDED FLIGHTS

"A bird does not sing because it has an answer.
It sings because it has a song."
CHINESE PROVERB

My flashlight was too weak to penetrate the darkness, but I told myself I wasn't afraid to walk alone in the black woods and stepped forward within a dim circle of light. Four hours and five cups of coffee earlier, I'd been working at my computer when the weather square of my welcome screen informed me that the Wisconsin winds were blowing at only one to two miles per hour at the Necedah National Wildlife Refuge. When the morning winds of late summer blow gently in this sanctuary, juvenile whooping cranes trail behind an ultralight plane as part of a program to reestablish a migrating Wisconsin-to-Florida flock.

Earlier in September, my son DJ and I had risen before sunrise to see the cranes. We squeezed the trip between our annual last-weekend-of-summer camping trip and DJ's first day of middle school. My husband worked the weekend, so DJ and I joined a dozen families from the neighborhood at adjacent campsites. If I didn't call it camping and just thought of it as a play weekend for the kids, I could stand the congestion, the giant slide emptying into a pool bubbling with screaming kids, and the cruise-ship-type activities. The official activity theme was "Halloween." DJ had rummaged through our costume box and found a plastic striped skirt and a pair of Dopey (Snow White's little dwarf with the elongated auricles) ears. He borrowed his older sister's Renaissance-looking cone-shaped hat with blue and pink scarves that fell from its tip in silken tresses and rested on the shoulders of his black T-shirt. The shirt sported a picture of Yoda pointing to a timeless imperative: "Pull My Finger." DJ called himself Princess Dopey, and he was a hit, getting may-I-take-my-picture-with-you-requests from kids and parents all over the Jellystone Resort. He and his buddies enjoyed the independence of juggling for lead position and riding their bikes in formation and in costume through the grounds. They checked in with parents between activities:

"We're going to play miniature golf."

"We want to swim now. Can one of the parents come to the pool?"

"They're showing cartoons at the outdoor theater. Do the little kids want to come?"

Sunday morning, everyone packed and lined up the trucks and cars for the drive home. When the convoy turned east, we turned west. DJ negotiated a plan for alternating control of the car music—Van Morrison, Switchfoot, Bob Dylan, Blink 182—while we moved closer to the part of Wisconsin that naturalist Aldo Leopold named "Sand County." Forests thinned, farms almost disappeared from the landscape, and I turned off the CD player. We entered Adams County and began to pass the castellated buttes and pinnacles that punctuated the scenery. DJ said he thought it looked as if they had once been islands, and I told him they had. A half billion years ago, sands slowly settled in a shallow Cambrian sea that covered much of the interior of North America. While most parts of the country compacted and cemented their silicone granulets under limestone and sedimentary layers, the Green Bay lobe of the Wisconsin Glacier excavated sand and gravel and dumped the icy load in this area. Fifteen thousand years ago, this heap of glacial scoopings dammed the outlet of the Wisconsin River and created the huge Lake Wisconsin, which covered parts of four counties. Waves pounded sandstone and quartzite, executing a suspension of sand and clay across the bed of the lake. As the climate warmed, the Wisconsin River muscled its way through weak Cambrian sandstone and laid a new course around the east hip of the Baraboo Hills, draining the immense glacial loch. The sandy soil of the former lakebed didn't allow any species of fauna or woodland flora to thrive in great numbers, so no type of forest or prairie dominated. Diversity became the prominent trait of the land. A wetland complex of swamps, meadows, and savannas emerged as a new habitat. Plant and animal species from northern and southern regions loosely took hold.

One of the most spectacular species to thrive here was the crane. Leopold described their morning appearance in his Wisconsin essay, "Marshland Elegy:"

"At last a glint of sun reveals the approach of a great echelon of birds. On motionless wing they emerge from the lifting mist, sweep a final arc of the sky and settle in clangorous descending spirals to their feeding grounds."

When Leopold wrote, only one type of crane lived in scant numbers in the area—the sandhill. He surely knew that the whooping crane was missing from the scene.

By 1884, three years before Leopold's birth, the migrating flocks of Midwest whooping cranes were lost to over-hunting and to the desecration of wetland habitats. There were only about two dozen whoopers alive by 1930, all wintering in Texas and migrating to an unknown location in Canada. No whooping cranes lived in or flew through Wisconsin.

We drove first to the Necedah Refuge and then found Grand Dike Road. At the end of an unnamed eyehook-shaped road, we found the last of three parking spaces. Our plan was to walk the trail so we would know the path in the dark morning of the next day. I'd never seen a whooping crane, the tallest bird in North America and the rarest crane in the world, and I imagined running behind Leopold, who led the way for a chance to see the reintroduced cranes. DJ picked up his pace to match mine and offered his encouragement: "Let's hurry so we have time to use the hot tub at the hotel before dinner."

Two hundred yards of wiggly trail led to an observation tower and to six admirers, hushed by the view. The tower stood in the trees but looked out toward the grassland, sedge meadow, wetland, and Ryerson

Pool (Lake). Two satin-white cranes foraged in and out of high grasses on tall legs that appeared to have backward bending knees. Through the binoculars, we could see the details of their black-tipped wings, folded and decorating their flanks as if they posed for a Japanese silk portrait.

DJ smiled sweetly at me. "Well, there they are. We saw them."

"Just give me a little time, hon'. We won't be long. I'd like to see them fly."

As if on cue, a mature crane unfolded its feathered scarf to seven feet of poise and received the wind. DJ pointed, "There one goes." As it soared, it began a vocalization that sounded like a turkey playing a harmonica. The call resonated from its five-foot-long trachea and filled the landscape. Black fringes on white wings skimmed across the sedges just before the crane dangled his feet to make a touch-and-go landing. He soared on a circular disk of lift in front of the tower, returned to the earth in a perfect spiral of descent, and landed in silence. I exhaled in unison with the other bird watchers.

DJ pulled the back of my shirt and reminded me "We'll be back in the morning." We hadn't been on the tower ten minutes, but I had promised we'd just take a quick look to get our bearings for the morning.

At the hotel, we alternated between hot tub and pool. In the pool, we raced. While in the hot tub, we talked about middle school and what to expect. He wanted to hear about my experiences: first dances, lunchroom cliques, and favorite classes. I remembered poems from a boy who'd developed a crush on me. "Your hair is fair; I wish your skin were bare."

"Did that really happen?"

"Yes. I still have the poems in a box somewhere. Even then, I knew they were funny enough to save."

We spent dinner making up bad poetry, "I patched the hole on your torn sleeve. I kissed you, and you didn't heave," bending into our plates and working to keep our laughter from becoming a dining spectacle.

That night, we both fell asleep quickly. When the clock read 4:44 a.m., I switched off the alarm, which was due in one minute. After I'd dressed, I pulled back the window curtain to find the end of night mantled in heavy rain. The weather forecast had promised clear skies. DJ sat up and saw my disgusted expression. I plopped on the bed. "It's pouring. You can go back to sleep."

Instead, DJ turned on the TV, and we watched the end of a Doris Day movie. Daylight began to peek into the room, and to our surprise, the rain stopped within an hour. We'd missed sunrise but hoped the cranes would train now that the weather seemed calm. DJ jumped out of bed, and in three minutes flat, he was at the door with all his belongings.

On the way to Necedah, he asked why the crane chicks don't just follow the adults who learned the way to Florida last year. I explained that when the decimation of the Midwest whoopers was complete, the migration pathway died out. These giants are territorial and don't follow unrelated cranes or fly in amassments like the sandhills. A flock is made up of small family groups that move from one area of the country to the same general geographic area, with no closer relationship than the human snowbirds of Racine might feel for the snowbirds of Green Bay. Each family in a migrating flock had to learn the way. Ornithologists tried placing whooper eggs with sandhill cranes, so the sandhills would raise the young and teach the route. That worked in so far as migration was concerned, but then the whooping cranes never imprinted on their own species and wouldn't mate. Whoopers raised by sandhills wouldn't mate with their own kind because they didn't understand what they were. The project was a bust.

The sandhills had recovered, in large part, by a national program of setting aside wetlands, which began with policies of Theodore Roosevelt and the creation of the US Forestry Service in 1905, and by Franklin D. Roosevelt, who founded the National Wildlife Refuge system in 1934. The government also made an attempt at controlling some trigger-fingers and loss of habitat in 1918. They passed the Migratory Bird Treaty Act Of 1918, which authorized the Secretary of Agriculture to protect migratory bird species, their eggs, and their nests. A Stanford University analysis predicts that one in ten bird species could vanish within 100 years. With losses in environmental protections over the last few years, the statistics are probably more grim than that study had predicted.

Whoopers, and nearly all crane species, have proved intolerant of civilization. The opposite is also true. Most people thought the whooping crane would never again fly or nest in their former homes in the wetlands of this ancient lakebed. In Patuxent, Maryland, where the Necedah chicks were hatched, and in other research centers, caretakers learned to cover up in white costumes and use a crane puppet on one hand to parent and imprint the markings of their species upon the chicks. Even though they were raising cranes since the 1960s, ornithologists had no idea how they'd reestablish a migratory flock.

They didn't yet know about a kid named Bill Lishman, who would grow up to indulge a childhood dream to soar with geese. Lishman's realized fantasy also provided an idea about a way to help birds reestablish lost migratory routes. He learned to fly and to modify his ultralight plane and to raise and imprint geese to follow him. In 1992, he flew a gaggle from Ontario to Virginia, and in the spring, the geese migrated back. Lishman proved that lost migratory routes could be reestablished. In 2000, he and a large support team led a flock sandhills from Necedah to central Florida. The next year, they led whooping cranes. An entire network of public and private foundations, the International Recovery Team with their specialists from Canada and the US, hope to build a flock of twenty-five breeding pairs.

A Civic Hybrid with a University of Wisconsin at Madison sticker was parked at the woodland lot, and its driver greeted us as we reached the top of the tower. A fiftyish man dressed in camouflage introduced himself and then his double-barreled, magnesium-alloy chassis, eight-by-forty-two Nikon binoculars, which he was willing to share. The commando bird watcher, Craig, pointed to the wetland and told us we were in luck.

A single whooping crane foraged through the sedges under a bright gray sky. Clouds swept by quickly, promising blue. We discussed the possibility of seeing the cranes fly. Craig was skeptical, telling us that the fast-moving clouds meant wind, but he wasn't giving up hope. "There's about a $100,000 tied up in each chick, and if it's windy, the cranes could crash into the ultralight. The reintroduction program has lost several like that over the last few years." He pointed to the pond where the chicks learned to spend the night in water. Bobcats are a big threat in Florida and regularly killed reintroduced whoopers before scientists trained the birds to head to the water for the evening. We both speculated that if cougars made a comeback in Wisconsin (cougars have been confirmed by the DNR in Upper Michigan—so close), the cranes' habit of sleeping in the water might also protect them from that predator as well. The price of teaching the cranes comes at a high price. One year, a sudden flood wiped out all of the season's whooping crane chicks, save one. The wild turkey, martin, and fisher thrive again in Northern Wisconsin after being evicted, along with the forests, over 100 years ago. Wisconsin again has forests and a flock of over 100 reintroduced trumpeter swans, but I'd never seen a trumpeter in the wild. Craig had, and he looked out to the lake and quoted the famous ornithologist, Edward Howe Forbush:

"In the glowing firmament rode the long baseless triangles of the Swans, sweeping across the upper air in exalted and unswerving flight, spanning a continent with the speed of the wind, their forms glistening like silver in the sunset glow. They presented the most impressive spectacle of bird life ever seen in North America."

I knew I would recall the quote when the day came for me to see the trumpeters. DJ looked back and forth between Craig and me, both of us staring at the one far-away crane. "Craniacs," he muttered, repeating the word he'd learned the day before. We left Craig and began our walk, agreeing that if we heard the engine of the ultralight, we could run back to the tower. As we began our hike through the oak pine forest and savanna, I sprung an idea on DJ, "Let's drive home through the Dells area and stop at the International Crane Foundation. They have all fifteen species of cranes in the world, and I've always wanted to go there."

DJ looked at me skeptically. "I don't want to miss football practice."

"It's only seven a.m. We've got time."

The rest of the hike, DJ considered venues, including Wizard World and the wax museum. He knew the Dells stop was a trade-off: one stupid attraction for him, and one tiresome bird sanctuary for me. I stooped to examine an array of wild mushrooms in blue, red, and yellow. "I've got to look these up when we get home."

"Oh, great. I see a mushroom book on your Christmas list already."

"Excellent idea."

"What's really weird about you is that you're not kidding." Suddenly distracted, he pointed behind me. "Look at those little pines over there with the sun hitting them."

Dew from the dawn rain glazed each white-pine needle in a fiber-optic brilliance. That's my boy, I thought. He's teasing me, but he notices the beauty of the earth. Whatever this joy was, he had an adolescent form of the addiction.

A lobe of Ryerson Pool formed a small bay in front of us, and through our binoculars, we saw a huge pen holding about five of this year's whooping cranes. They had outgrown most of the caramel in their chick plumage and wore the elegant penna of their parents. Two adult whoopers, who had grown in these pens in previous summers, loitered statuesquely near the cage. DJ spotted the black mustache and red patch on the forehead of one of the adults. Most species of cranes have a red patch that flushes to show excitement or territorial intimidation. Aldo Leopold wrote of the cranes as "wilderness incarnate." DJ directed me to find the bird with my binoculars and wondered out loud how the cranes ended up in this spot.

Necedah is the largest refuge in Wisconsin, about 45,000 acres, and almost all of it is perfect crane country. Leopold worked on the Wild Life Restoration Committee that recommended the system of refuges. This refuge was established in 1939, while Leopold was advising FDR about lands to acquire for the refuge system. The land here was too sandy to grow vigorous crops, so farmers sold their poorly producing fields back to the government. The Restoration Committee member who wrote the recommendation was Jay "Ding" Darling. We'd visited the Ding Darling refuge on Sanibel Island in Florida and seen white pelicans, roseate spoonbills, and alligators. DJ remembered me picking him up to hurry past the seven-foot sleeping gator, and he remembered the silly name "Ding." Darling had made his living as an editorial cartoonist and signed his cartoons with the first letter and last three letters of his last name. In addition to his Pulitzer-winning cartoons and committee work to establish the National Wildlife Refuge system, Darling founded the Federal Duck Stamp Program and the National Wildlife Federation.

DJ wouldn't let me look at more mushrooms, and he was talking about bacon and eggs as we climbed the observation tower one more time to check out the crane activity. About eight white spots moved slowly near the horizon, and Craig updated us on the action: "No flying today—too windy. The cranes just appeared way out there and haven't flown." He encouraged us to borrow his high-powered binoculars, showing us how to use our trigger fingers to focus on the wading birds and the pond that hadn't been visible without his super scope. DJ's stomach rumbled as he took his turn with Craig's binoculars, so when he returned the glasses and looked at me, I nodded permission to leave and watched him start for the stairs.

In town, the Coffee Haus Pizza Café drew us from the street with smells of coffee and bacon. DJ chose his stupid Dells activity around a gray aluminum-edged table that filled with breakfast food as we talked. He wanted to see the Ripley's museum and also pleaded to complete the experience by buying a useless souvenir, arguing, "What's a stupid attraction without a crappy keepsake?" I was an easy mark but set a $5 limit. A malediction printed above Ripley's entranceway warned that the spectacle of the copyrighted museum cannot be revealed under penalty of curse. DJ shortly declared the gift shop "lame," so we stopped at a 50 percent off souvenir shop where he bought a light-up jester hat. He wore the jester hat to our next stop, the International Crane Foundation in Baraboo—the only place in the world to see all fifteen species of cranes, most of them existing on the precarious edge of survival. We toured with a naturalist, but the real work of the ICF wasn't in the tour area. The off-limits Crane City serves to raise cranes in the solitude they crave and to fulfill their mission to preserve and defend all species of cranes and their habitats. The foundation spreads its influence to the five continents that host the fifteen types. They lobby and educate for preservation of land with hopes to reestablish populations and migratory routes and work toward achieving the genetic diversity in the chicks and flocks of the world.

One of the ICF founders, Dr. George Archibald, bonded with a whooper who carried genetic codes from a flock that no longer existed. The crane, "Tex," had imprinted on a dark-haired zoo worker who raised her, and now she looked to dark-haired men as potential mates. Dr. George Archibald moved into the crane's living environment at ICF and learned to impress his partner in an interactive mating dance: necks extended, arms thrown back as they lifted up off the ground. They jumped up and traveled a gentle arc before landing as softly and proudly as a pair of ballet dancers. He must have felt silly as he pranced, but she responded by displaying the rubescent excitement of her head patch, and she laid an egg. It took six years for her to lay a fertile egg that was successfully inseminated and incubated. For each of those six years, Archibald spent the spring dancing with Tex. Although Tex was killed by a predator shortly after her offspring was born, the chick ("Gee Whiz") carried the genetic line to subsequent generations of birds who live free in a non-migratory Florida flock. The ICF has bred each of the fifteen rare crane species and has begun reintroduction and preservation programs all over the world, including Russia, Thailand, Africa, North America, and India.

Twelve of the fifteen crane species were caged in one big circle cut into pie wedges by gray walls. Each wedge held a pair of birds. The naturalist asked us not to speak to the cranes nor call nor imitate their cries. The first and largest crane, the sarus, walked up to the fence and lowered his head and flushed red at DJ. My senses had dulled to DJ's startling crimson-lit jester hat, but his head gear and his red "I live in my own little world. It's okay, they know me here" T-shirt transformed my son into a master crane intimidator. His get-up was interpreted as a threat by the territorial cranes. DJ turned off his hat as we hurried away, and the sarus cranes, the world's tallest flying bird, demonstrated their soft, smoky call.

Each type of crane represented its species' tale of woe in our narrated walk around the cages. The southeastern Asia subspecies of sarus barely survived the environmental disasters of war in Korea and Vietnam, and now their populations dwindle in the presence of pesticides and fertilizers and the human population's demand for more and more of their habitat. We heard the history of humanity's desecration of the species that had once required nothing but space and solitude and now require interactive cooperation from five continents to be afforded the privilege of existence in marginal numbers in their natural habitat. In Africa's Cape Province and Orange Free State, all of their wattled cranes are gone, and wattled populations are declining everywhere in the continent, along with the wetlands.

The red crowned crane, whose dancing image inspires oriental poetry, mythology, and art, breed in the Amur River basin near the China-Russia border. This second rarest crane in the world is being squeezed out of China and Japan as development reduces the habitat available to the endangered birds. The third rarest crane, the Siberian, is caught in a political dilemma. The largest flock had wintered in the mudflats of Poyang Lake in China. Annual flooding in eastern China transformed the flats into a seasonal lake, but the Three Gorges Dam on the Yangtze River despoiled the habitat. China decided to provide hydroelectric power for 18.2 million Chinese homes without regard to the 3,000 cranes dependent on the habitat. That is not surprising considering 1.3 million people were displaced when the dam project took their land. I wish there were a different option for the people and the cranes. The State-owned dam has been called "the world's most notorious dam" because of economic corruption and escalating environmental impact. Consequences include massive mudslides, pressure induced seismic activity, decreased phytoplankton, and a resultant collapse of the fishing industry that had sustained millions. Biodiversity has decreased with big losses for the paddlefish and Chinese sturgeon. The Baijin river dolphin is now considered functionally extinct. The losses and suffering are so great that the cranes hardly get a mention.

Each story of environmental despair had a ray of hope. ICF helped to persuade the South Korean government to preserve the Han River estuary for the white naped, red crowned, and hooded cranes. A Russian ICF ornithologist, Dr. Sergei Smirenski, helped to establish the first privately operated nature park in Russia in the crane habitat of the Amur River Basin. The ingenuity of the ICF made me want to believe in the power of conservationists to undo a measure of damage and reclaim the birthright of the cranes.

DJ slept all the way home and told his dad that night, "We saw over fifteen different whooping cranes today, and at one time, there were only that many pairs alive in the world." DJ didn't seem disappointed about not seeing the juveniles fly with the utralights, perhaps because he didn't want to be subjected to another pre-dawn rising. I watched the weather reports and reported wind velocity every day.

My family was asleep when I made my middle-of-the-night decision a few weeks later. I tapped my husband on the shoulder, explained my plan, and reassured him, "Don't worry. If I get tired, I'll pull over to a wayside and sleep." Walking down the hall to my son, I hoped he would ask to come along, which would mean missing sleep and school. The pros and cons bantered in my head, but DJ didn't ask to join me. Like his dad, he told me to be careful, accepted my kiss, and went back to sleep.

I arrived in the woods outside the Necedah marsh forty-five minutes before dawn and hesitated, suddenly thinking I'm-a-woman-alone-in-the-woods thoughts that served no practical purpose once I was alone in the woods. I assigned my keys, thermos of hot coffee, and limbs secondary roles as weapons, aimed the flashlight a few inches ahead of my feet, and moved through my fear. When Leopold wrote of those who arrive "too soon early in the marsh," he observed, "like many another treaty of restraint, the pre-dawn pact lasts only as long as darkness humbles the arrogant."

The feel of the smooth wooden rail of the tower felt like the beginning of safety, and my worries stayed below the bottom stair. Shimmering stars pulled my gaze upward. A river of hazy light, formed by a distal swirl of our spiral galaxy, snatched my attention. Within a half hour, the Milky Way dissolved into the waning night. Unruly thrashing in the trees didn't concern me. I'd learned from previous startles that the most riotous animals in the trees were squirrels and chipmunks. Mourning doves began to coo the rest of the marsh awake; a musical clamoring of honking cranes finished the job. As if on a dimmer switch, a blue light softy lit the grass below, but the bulk of the marsh held tight to its blanket of dense cloud. The blue fog covered all but the tips of three oaks, which appeared as the first dabs of an impressionist painting.

The grasses below sent up their wet hay smell, musky and sweet. I decided it was still too early to worry that I'd miss the training flight again. A white-breasted nuthatch appeared at my eye level and perched upside-down in a white pine. Blue-gray wings and a black cap contrasted neatly with its white chest. Chickadees chanted their name and poked in the bark for insects. Chickadees and nuthatches spend a lot of time together when they are not mating and rearing. They like the same habitat, and since one searches the bark while upright and one pecks while topsy-turvy, they explore different crevices of the tree and don't compete with each other.

In the grasses ahead, a flash of brown and yellow. A female red-winged blackbird scurried forward and vanished into the blue bank. From the fog, a dry cry turned into a sloppy round of calls as dozens of rusty-gray sandhills began their day. An even louder, more melodic series of gobbling clamors came from the eleven-o'clock position where I knew some of the whoopers were caged. The other pen, which DJ and I had hiked to see, was behind me at five o' clock, and that brood answered in a sudden uproar. They seemed to call the sun and the daylight. The morning's blue fog luminesced and contracted, revealing a new strip of grassland. I zeroed in on what looked like a sunflower, but through my binoculars, I saw it was an endangered compass plant. Its foliage forms large lobes that align themselves north-south in the daylight so that their broad leaves are not exposed to the strong south-facing sun.

A couple of birdwatchers with long binoculars and bird books in hand joined me on the tower, whispering "Oh, no—fog." They began looking around, asking me what I'd seen. As we inspected the landscape, a flock of fifteen sandhills flew in formation over us, arching away from the tower, the undersides of their wings copper in the dawn light. The lifting fog exposed more grassland and just a bit of marsh. The three of us and our six binocular eyes observed the morning.

"Three deer at two o' clock."

"The dark flock heading to the pond are cormorants."

"One, two, three, four undulations in the flight pattern of that woodpecker—it's a pileated. A beauty."

"Can't mistake that call. There it is—a blue jay."

By seven-thirty, we could see Ryerson Pool. Rotating in circles of viewing with woods behind us, oak savanna to our left, marshland and pond ahead, we spotted woodcocks, red-breasted grosbeaks, barn swallows, horned grebes, many flocks of sandhills, a pair of lesser scaups, a dozen wild turkeys, a harrier hawk (that quieted the songbirds down for a bit), and more. Mr. Birdwatcher wasn't sure but thought he heard a black-billed cuckoo. None of us were skilled enough to tell the warblers apart, so we didn't know how many different kinds we'd seen. We heard and saw three times as many birds and wildlife as I would have seen by myself. Well after sun-up, no whoopers had shown.

The couple started to leave. "I'm not sure," I told them, "but I think I hear an engine. I wouldn't leave yet."

Mrs. Birdwatcher looked doubtful. "That can't be an ultralight," she said. "Wouldn't that loud engine scare the chicks?"

"All these eggs were hatched in Maryland's Patuxent Wildlife Refuge." I explained that they play a recording of the engine to the eggs, and keep playing for the chicks so they remain accustomed to the noise. The handlers and trainers all wear the same identically-styled white costume. They cover all their human features and carry a crane puppet with the white head, red crown, and black mustache. So, we waited.

An ultralight flew over the marsh, looking like a giant-hinged kite with a ghost in its tiny chassis. No cranes followed. I quickly conjectured, "I read they fly with at least two planes when they migrate. The pilot can't see the whole flock. They must train that way too."

Finally, just after eight a.m., six juvenile whooping cranes—the most ancient of our living bird species—followed an ultra-light out into the open sky above the marsh. A caramel tint softened the hue of their white feathers and differentiated their plumage from mature birds. Their trusting pursuit and willowy outstretched necks evoked a tender feeling toward the vulnerable young. More than thirty cranes from years of previous training had found their way back to this land on their own. Our eyes never left the miracle of a human acting like a bird. The whoopers caught the updraft from the warmth of the thick vegetation near the colder water and rode it up and away, circling back toward us and right over our heads. Tranquil wings stretched wide as the juveniles put their trust in a white-costumed pilot who leaned a puppet crane out of the cockpit.

I lingered alone, long enough to see two tiny Karner blue butterflies alight simultaneously on the corner of the tower. I'd never seen one of these endangered butterflies. Their one-inch wingspan flaunted deep royal blue wings with pale white-spotted undersides. The larva of the small butterfly feeds only on lupine, and the symbiotic pair flourishes in the nearby sunny oak savanna. How kind the butterflies were to come to me. The wilderness before me was only to be viewed from this tower. A sign at the base announced the territory in the viewing area ahead of the tower as "off limits." I agreed. Better we stand out of the way and leave the cranes and the land alone. Let the professional naturalist intervene when necessary, because the nearby development couldn't coexist with the wide-scale fires that had managed the savanna for the previous 13,000 years. These birds don't want to see us. American nature lovers and adventurers seek the wild: climb the virgin mountain summit, borrow an ax and go live off the land, and fish the streams where the trout have never seen a hand-tied fly. Most want to blaze their own trail and step off the path. The nature lover who stands at the edge of an unmolested habitat and chooses to withhold her footprints recognizes that she has already taken too much from the land and that there are too many of us for too little wilderness.

On the way back home, I stopped twice for short naps and coffee and had time to think about the morning. I hadn't made an effort to see the diminutive Karner blue butterfly. In typical American fashion, I'd sought the newest, the most ancient, and the rarest. If we love the cranes enough to save their environment, thousands of other species will flourish and avoid extinction. We seem programmed to save what we aesthetically love. The beauty of the cranes captivated me, just as they have always inspired humanity. Leopold said, "Our ability to perceive quality in nature begins, as in art, with the pretty." Images of cranes decorate ancient oriental silks, prehistoric African caves, and imaginations around the world. Crane *likenesses* are indeed more plentiful than the live version.

The image of a wild whooping crane flock in the Midwest is nearly a reality. For the first time in 100 years, pairs of migratory whooping cranes have raised their chicks in the eastern US. The cranes have not yet learned to be good parents and lose many eggs and chicks to predation. Every year that the nonprofit group, Operation Migration, nurtures the chicks and prods them to reanimate the ancient flyway, they increase the prospect that wild whoopers will hatch in former Wisconsin breeding grounds and will then learn the migration route from their actual crane family. These could be the first chicks to depend on their parents to teach them the route and begin to make Lishman and his ultralight an obsolete accessory to a natural process. No one knows if any will survive their first year, including the winter and migratory passages. In spring, those who love wildness will be perking their ears and craning their necks, seeking the return of these first wild whoopers of a new ornithological age. The Wisconsin-to-Florida flock exists because a refuge in Canada, originally set aside for buffalo, serendipitously provided a breeding ground for the last small flock of whooping cranes that migrated to Aransas National Wildlife Refuge in Texas. Ornithologists, noting cranes tend to lay two eggs but nurture only one, plucked one egg from each nest and worked to save and breed the cranes. It took over thirty years of dancing, costumes, puppets, and ultralight flights to come to the brink of a new migratory flock, and this is only a sketch of efforts toward one of the crane species' recovery efforts.

Henry David Thoreau didn't seem to foresee how complicated the work would be before we could see our rare winged beauty riding the seasonal winds in their elegant black and white plumes when he wrote, "When I detect a beauty in any of the recesses of nature, I am reminded, by the serene and retired spirit in which it requires to be contemplated, of the inexpressible privacy of a life, how silent and unambiguous it is." Silence does interpret nature, but so do literature, laughter, science, and camaraderie. Preserving the beauty that we love, even if it is only for our selfish pleasure, will require us to be creative, ambitious, diplomatic, cooperative, brilliant, sacrificing, and to plug into our playful spirits that are willing to be foolish. That blue bank of fog had pulled back slowly enough to show me that saving the crane was saving everything.

Once home, I fell asleep while dropping to the bed. Two hours later, the front door opened, and DJ yelled up the stairs, "Yo, Mama, what *is* up, home slice?" He climbed the stairs asking if I saw the cranes train with the ultralights. He wanted to know if my trip was worth my middle-of-the-night drive. I told him about the birds, ducks, butterflies, and fragile life I saw in the refuge. In the land beyond the tower, the habitat seethed with more life than I could comprehend. He lay down next to me and turned away. It was a signal we both understood through years of imprinting, and I rolled toward him to scratch his back.

VALLEY OF THE SNAKE

*"Where, after all, do universal human rights begin?
In small places, close to home— so close and so small
that they cannot be seen on any maps of the world."*
ELEANOR ROOSEVELT

I wanted to whisk my son away to share the clear breath of autumn upon a wide river before the winter winds would come to brandish us
with chilling drafts. The dramatic geology, hardwood forests, and waters of
the Wisconsin Dells called. Experience had taught me that after a private
hour with DJ, my name changes from the two-syllable Ma…oom, back to
Mom. With his middle-school guard down, I hoped the Dells would offer
up its lesson to him about the tendency of people to divert, steal, and ruin
resources and to help him appreciate the effect of the man and family who
saved what is still beautiful about the Dells. H.H. Bennett and his family
lived Rachel Carson's words from *Silent Spring* long before she wrote them.
"The more clearly we can focus our attention on the wonders and realities
of the universe about us, the less taste we shall have for destruction."

Twelve-year-old Amber had never seen the Wisconsin River, so I
couldn't say "no" when she asked to join us on our boat trip and nature
walk, even though I had to drum up a happy voice to tell her "Sure, you
can come along." I'm a volunteer mentor to Amber, who lives near the
Milwaukee neighborhood where I'd raised my daughter as a single parent
when my first husband took leave of his family. During the short drive to
the central city, I tried to push away my resentment about the change in

our day as I attempted to cheer up my sullen, though uncomplaining, son. "We'll have a fun day. You know how she likes you."

Amber is black, a year older than DJ, and enjoys his quick-to-be-silly personality. DJ is white and at the developmental age where he is resistant to being around girls of any race. Still, he knew to offer our guest the front seat of our car, and he pretended to be relieved when I briefed Amber on our route and handed her the map. He told her, "You have to be navigator when you sit there—Mom's rule."

Amber looked up at me. I tried to read her emotion. Was I putting too much pressure on her; did she understand that we weren't going to get lost? I reviewed the route with her several times as we sat in front of her small home that her grandmother had called "raggedy" the first time she gave me directions and a description. When Amber traced the route with her fingers and named the roads, I knew she understood. She directed me to Interstate 94 West. When we passed Johnson's Creek, I asked her to tell me about the next two turns and then suggested she could sleep if she wished. We had over an hour to go, and her grandmother had told me she'd been awake since five a.m., eager for our seven a.m. pick-up.

Both children slept as our car turned north and passed the Baraboo Hills. A multicolored October coat covered the worn-down mountains of Baraboo quartzite in a patchwork of green, gold, and red. More than five million years ago, this continent floated over the equator. After volcanic diastrophisms had pushed edges of the earth's crust into mountains, these ancient hills were tall peaks that towered over tropical land and sea. If I had made my sleeping passengers wake up and had taken them up to these 800-foot-high hills, I'd have shown them the ripples in the quartzite rock that look just like perfect wavelets in the sand, because that is what they were at one time. The inland sea deposited the sand, and time had cooked it. I'd have asked them why the two billion-year-old little waves were without blemish. Don't worms, clams, fish, and other life usually disrupt the surface of the sand? Hadn't DJ and I seen the miniscule holes of the augers reappear after every wave erased them in the sand of Mexico, Florida, California, and every other ocean beach we'd seen? It would have been fun to see their faces when they figured out that these unsullied furrows were made before any marine life existed. The only form of life on the planet at that time were bacteria, laboring in ignorance on their one-and-half-billion-year project to oxygenate the planet and to provide a protective ozone shield for more complicated life forms of the future.

Amber had never seen the town of Wisconsin Dells and awoke to a huge billboard of Paul Bunyan waving at her, followed by an alarmingly yellow roller coaster, and the Volcano Miniature Golf course—all the gaudiness of Las Vegas without the imposing architecture. "What's that?" she asked quietly at each enticement and politely withheld requests to enjoy any of the carnivalesque attractions. I told her we were going to see something better, and neither DJ in the back seat nor Amber in the front seat disputed me in words. In their not-so-secret desires, the bewitchments, marketed to appear as instant fun, called to them. I did feel privileged to have the respect and trust of these quickly growing children and hoped they would find fascination in the natural and unusual sights ahead. Since many of the big attractions were closed for the season, they gave themselves over to my plans without complaint.

Whenever someone tells me they know Wisconsin because they've visited the Dells, I cringe at the thought of their association with our state being tied to the touristy town of Wisconsin Dells. Will the life-sized troll who belts out Louis Armstrong's, "What a Wonderful World" or the caricature artist with his slogan "No Face Too Ugly" or the water parks, or the fudge shops be the image they take away from Wisconsin? Most kids talk their parents into taking the Lower Dells tour where they can ride the wild amphibious car-boats—the ducks. They remember the fun of driving and splashing into the river and comment briefly on some interesting cliffs. Some miss the intimate interaction and visceral appreciation of the Dells' unusual natural assets seen in the river valley of the upper Dells— or maybe they don't miss it at all. Maybe they come for a good time, and that's enough for some. I wanted to be sure that DJ and Amber knew about this land and the ancient desert and glacier action that had sculpted this river valley, which had initially been the tourist draw of the Dells. I wanted them to understand the original enchantment of this place.

Long before the ancient seas or glaciers covered any of North America, an immense desert circled the rocky peaks of Canada and filled much of the continent. The desert sands were granules of tumbled quartzite, blasted by strong winds when there was no plant life to anchor anything to the earth. Without plants or oxygen, the earth had no ozone layer to protect any elements from the bleaching and sterilizing effects of the full spectrum of powerful radiation from the sun, so the quartzite sand was severely white. When the sea level rose, the Baraboo Mountains were the only peaks that rose above the waves for hundreds of miles. The oceans eventually left the land; continents migrated; and millions of years later, glaciers from the north took dominion over land and life. The tons of ice stopped just short of the Dells and Baraboo Hills. Glaciers never touched the southwestern part of Wisconsin.

We found the boat tour ticket office and had only a short wait. While in line, Amber touched DJ's elbow to pull him back to read his T-shirt, knowing he usually wore something silly. The dancing rodents and "Squirrels Gone Wild" caption didn't disappoint.

We were warned about the lack of restrooms on the boat, so we all made a stop at the shore facilities. I teased DJ when we met up with him again. "Our bathroom had velvet couches and free chocolate covered cherries in the formal lounge." DJ remembered when he used to go into ladies' rooms with me and had lamented the injustice of women sometimes having nicer restrooms. I'd clued Amber in on our game but didn't know if she'd play along. In her family, she suffers from an insufficiency of adult attention because the adult-to-child ratio of availability is not in her favor. Her elderly grandmother raises her and five other grandchildren. Amber usually adjusts slowly to my playful attention.

DJ countered, "We had ramps and skateboards, and I made a 360 jump, landed in front of the urinal, hit the bull's-eye painted on the porcelain back, won $50,000, and gave it all to charity."

Amber chimed in, "We had seat belts and went on an action ride while we did our business."

She swung her arms as we walked toward the boat landing. Our concrete path forked into stairs and a ramp. Amber took the ramp and playfully let the momentum propel her into a fun run. "Wooooweee," she called, flitting down close to but not into a crowd of women. They backed away from her. The dirty looks were brief. I quickly picked up my pace and copied her "Wooooweee" in a little softer tone, wrapped my arm around her shoulder, and led her gently away toward the line of benches. DJ followed—minus the yell and the attention. Amber was the only black person waiting for this boat. In addition to this irregularity, she'd broken some perceived social rules and been a little too loud and a little too close to others. I couldn't be sure if it was my imagination that the crowd seemed indignant, or if they were reacting non-discriminatingly to what they saw as inappropriate wildness. I did feel our difference as the shifting eyes of several other boaters moved over us. Amber asked if we could change our seats and move out of the sun.

As we moved, I tried to dispel my discomfort, focusing instead on the seventy-degree warmth of the day. "Doesn't the sun feel good?"

She whispered to me, "I get too black."

We all put on sunscreen in preparation to sit on the exposed deck of the boat. I whispered to Amber that I thought she had beautiful skin as I squirted a dab of lotion to her hand and watched her rub it onto her forehead and cheeks. She answered, "That's what my grandma tells me." Her face had a deep matte finish and eyes that seemed to absorb everything but seldom reflected emotion back. Her teachers called her slow, but I knew she'd never been given the attention, stimulation, and resources that my son enjoyed. She didn't even have the resources my daughter had enjoyed. Although our little family had been quite poor, my Andrea grew up with a mother who believed that our poverty was temporary—and it was. I took it for granted that I would be able to build, not an American dream of riches but rather, a life of hard work that would yield self-satisfaction and a degree of security.

Amber sat very close to me and picked at her cuticles. Her shoulder-length hair was pulled back into a ponytail. "You were smart to pull your hair back," I told her. "I'm going to do the same thing." As we walked to the boat, *The Yellow Thunder*, I gathered my hair like hers.

DJ deferred to Amber. "You take the seat on the outside. It has the best view."

The guide on board began to tell us about the area as we moved down a Cimmerian river dwarfed by towering sandstone cliffs. Little jugs, which I recognized as nests from cliff swallows, dotted the face of the bluff. The swallows had already left for South America as the frosty autumn nights had killed off their insect dinners or sent them into hibernation.

The creamy yellowed cliffs, white sand colored in the patinas of millennia, offered a distinct contrast to the tannin-dyed river that originated in the tamarack swamps in northwest Wisconsin. Pine, hemlock, and yellow birch crowded the upper ledges and protruded as if about to topple dramatically down the cliff. These were the trees of the northern forests that don't usually appear en masse this far south. These trees were descended from woods that lived beside the glaciers. When the Ice Age withdrew, the trees stayed.

DJ and Amber turned their heads to the right as *The Yellow Thunder* hugged the northeast bank of the river. The cliffs of High Rock towered more than 100 feet above our heads. Chimney rock emerged as stacked slabs of flat, yellow rock, demonstrating the origin of the name of this region (*Dalles* is French for "flat layered rock"). Just before the bright light of the blue sky dimmed in response to the shadows of the high cliffs, we passed a formation in the cliff—a stony profile named Black Hawk. The Wisconsin River had to deepen to 100 feet and turn on its side at the narrows to squeeze through the fifty-foot wide channel. As we traveled in shade, our guide told us the rays of the sun had never touched the floor of a narrow dry gorge just east of the canyon.

We all looked toward the flash of light above when the river momentarily widened and narrowed. We heard the legend of Black Hawk as we flowed through the narrows. Our guide used the word "relocated" to describe the government's attempts to herd the Sauk tribe westward across the Mississippi. The Sauk Indians had never lived in the Dells, but their Chief incited his horse to jump this span of river when trying to escape from the US soldiers. Our guide didn't elaborate how Black Hawk and his tribe fought back and suffered devastating losses, so I whispered the parts of the story I knew. When the Sauk Chief saw he could not regain his land, he sent bearers of white flags to admit defeat to the soldiers of

General Atkinson. The US Army attacked. They claimed they didn't understand the intent to surrender and opened fire on the Sauk families. After killing hundreds, the Army declared victory at what is now known as the Bad Axe Massacre.

History tells us that eventually, Black Hawk fled into the wilds of "the Dalles." While the story of the jump may or may not be true, archives of local newspapers confirm that the Winnebago Indians captured him in this area and traded him to the US government for $100 and twenty horses. For a year, Black Hawk was paraded around the country as a living trophy. He died in 1838. James Jordan, a white man, dug up Black Hawk's Iowa grave, cut the head off the corpse, and exhibited the body in pieces. He then burned the rotting flesh from the bones so he could continue to display the skeletal remains. The Iowa Governor insisted on the return of the Black Hawk bones and had them transported to an Iowa museum. Black Hawk's bones finally received the dignity of final rest only when there was not a scrap left of him that could be exploited. The museum burned to cinders, and his ashes were too small to carry any identity.

The three of us sat in the dark shade with hunched shoulders, and the kids leaned into me as I told the story. Amber asked if it was really true, and when I said "Yes," DJ commented that the guide had only told the legend of the jump; they'd skipped the truth.

As we passed into the wide span of river just past Black Hawk Island, the calm water began to look like a long lake. The breeze chilled, and the air, which had smelled like a cave in the damp narrows, turned crisp.

The Yellow Thunder moved toward the wide cleft called Witches Gulch. The chasm brought us to a boat dock and to a wooden-planked boardwalk suspended about twenty feet above the base of an undulating gulch. In some places, the cliffs almost joined, leaving only a foot of space between the two bluffs. In other places, the rocks opened into a natural cathedral lit from above. Below the walkway, a trout stream swirled noisily, echoing up the chamber walls. Mosses, lichens, and ferns grew from the sodden sandstone. Sweet pine above the cleft slid fragrance down the gulch. Deeper in, where the narrowing seemed oppressive, the dark, cramped passageway was appropriately named "Spooky Lane."

The kids had to come back for me because I lingered at some blobs of orange and yellow discolorations surrounded by green mosses. Instead of pulling me away (great kids!) they leaned toward the objects of my attention. Moss and lichen specimens lay before us on a ledge. The colorful blobs were lichens, one of the longest living species, some estimated to be 4,500 years old. When Moses and his Israelite followers found large vegetative flakes on the desert sand, they cooked it into bread and called it "manna." DJ told me that at nearby Devil's Lake, his Scout Master taught him that the name of one of the mosses before us. It was pine moss. Amber and I moved our faces only inches from the mounds of green carpet, and each little stalk of moss did look like a miniaturized pine tree. I looked at Amber's eyes, searching the diminutive life, and I saw her satisfaction when she said, "Oh, yeah. I see the teeny trees."

We walked ahead and touched the cool canyon walls that had been carved by rushing waters. Some say the canyons were carved over eons, but most geologists from Madison now believe that when the glacial dam that plugged the Wisconsin River let loose, the ancient Lake Wisconsin drained violently and created these sandstone valleys and the new riverbed in only weeks, or even days.

The boardwalk terminated at a large canyon dominated by a snack and souvenir shop. We all poked around, but I noticed Amber stayed very close to me. We were still with the same boat group, and it did feel as if they'd stopped staring at us. One employee, a white-haired woman, kept her eyes aimed at us to the exclusion of doing anything else. This time, I watched back, trying to identify if I was being hyper-sensitive or if Amber was being scrutinized as a potential thief.

I decided not to buy anything, but lingered with Amber, examining everything that caught her interest. DJ wandered around on his own, attracting no interest from anyone. Amber and I bent over a series of postcards that were reproductions from the artist who made the Dells famous. H.H. Bennett was the renowned landscape photographer who created the tourist interest in this area when he captured stunning representations for the then popular stereograph. The picture-viewing device used two photographs taken from slightly different angles to create a spatial and perspectual effect that vividly conveyed the crags and chasms of the Dells. He loved this area and had been the first non-native to enter Witches Gulch.

H.H. Bennett was a naturalist before the term was invented. His fascination with the unusual beauty of the land and water and his belief that it should be preserved filled his life with purpose. Because his wife, Francis, learned to run the portrait studio from which the family derived their steady income, he was free to develop his landscape photography business. After Francis died, his second wife, Evelyn, asked to learn to take the portraits so he'd be free to pursue his passion.

Amber and I bent into the circular rack and noticed that some of the pictures didn't look like today. "Landing at Witches Gulch" showed a cave-like formation at the entrance that we hadn't seen. The cliffs looked taller, and the river narrower. Were the pictured formations at another landing?

We walked back to the boat and reexamined the impressive formations all the way. Amber, who had dragged one finger along the canyon wall as we walked out, turned around to look into the deep rift. Her arms hung at her side, but her right wrist flexed up and waved goodbye to the novel grandeur of the rocks. DJ confidently walked ahead to the boat. He didn't seem to wonder if he'd ever return. While he had an appreciation of the place, he took the opportunity to see nature's wonderment for granted. It wasn't just a matter of an austerity versus richness of experiences in his life; he had a mindset of big possibilities. DJ believed that he would be able to access a fair share of the resources of the world, and it seemed to me likely that he would grow both to claim and work toward his goals confidently. He saw himself as a good guy, not afraid of hard work, capable, and he saw himself with a hopeful future. I celebrated his certitude and ached to support this confidence in Amber. She lived five miles away from me in a world that I could only partially understand. I'd been poor and put myself through college as a single parent while working full-time. It took every bit of energy and resources I possessed to succeed. There had been a time in my life when I thought that if I could pull myself out of poverty, anyone could do it. Looking back at those arduous days of anguished responsibility, I came to understand that I could not have succeeded if one more obstacle or responsibility had burdened me. If at the time I'd had two children, a needy sister, a boss who wouldn't change my shift hours when my class schedule changed each semester, if I wasn't a fast reader or if I struggled in math, if I was intimidated by financial aid forms, or if I wasn't sure I could succeed—any one of these barriers might have stopped me. Years later, when I worked in the inner city as a home health nurse, I got a close-up look at the unrelenting obstacles to daily living where poverty infests culture. Amber's gaze into the Witches Gulch hinted at an unexpressed longing. I couldn't help but be aware that while DJ played three instruments, Amber had to drop out of her choral group because she didn't have a reliable ride to practice. She never thought to call me to ask for help. DJ's teacher summoned my husband and me to school when she noticed that our son had trouble pronouncing R's. Amber's teachers haven't ever returned my calls about my desire to help her with her school problems. Her grandma gave me a confidentiality release, and I have called at least once a week for three months. I've spoken to her teachers and the school social worker only when I've reached them directly—about three out of twenty tries. Despite several meetings at her school, the teaching support staff fails to amend her assignments to make them comprehensible for her, as her learning plan calls for. Her reading ability, three levels below grade expectations, just doesn't appear to register as a priority to her teachers where violence and low performance are endemic in a district with a measly 36 to 50 percent graduation rate, depending on who calculates the statistics. Amber's performance at school meets expectations because she has good attendance and she behaves herself.

Two adults with education and interests in science, literature, nature, sports, gardening, swimming, biking, history, science, travel and more surround DJ with stimulation. Amber's household is headed by one determined and loving elderly grandmother, focused on meeting the challenges of the day. Fifty years after Brown v. Board of Education of Topeka declared segregation unconstitutional, Amber shares her classroom with only one Caucasian, while DJ enjoys the diversity of about 65 percent white students and the rest a mix of African American, Chinese, Hmong, Indian, and other races. Of the two, he's the one who benefits from desegregation.

Amber pulled me out of these thoughts by looking to the boat and then to me and then to the boat. She walked with me to join DJ, whispering more to herself than me, "That was cool."

Our guide called the broad river a "bay." We crossed the wide water in a marked lane to another landing. A rock formation, hundreds of feet up in the air, framed two circular bits of blue sky. The Demon's Anvil served as a marker for the next walk. Past the anvil, we gathered at the base of a rimrock platform layered atop the pillar and standing about seven feet away from a main cliff ledge. The air between these two lithic structures had made history. Stand Rock was the site where Bennett proved the worth of his invention, the stop-action camera. He had his son, Ashley, leap to Standing Rock repeatedly until his shutter caught the image of the action at just the midpoint. After eighteen attempts, Bennett snapped the picture, which now resides in the Smithsonian. Bennett's camera captured the spontaneity of a jump, a smile, and a personality and changed how we view history by putting an end to the five-minute stiff pose, which had been the photographic norm.

Ho-Chunk natives used to gather at a small glen to the south of these formations, and until a decade ago, they continued their ceremonial dances here. This had been their sacred land, formed when the Great Spirit took the form of a snake and slithered through stone as his pounding heart melted ice and split rock. His great jaws opened and spat forth deer, bear, turkey, and sturgeon. The Ho-Chunk stopped regular performances of their ceremonial dances to give more time to their casinos. My first inclination was to lament this shift, as if performing their spiritual dances on cue for boats of tourists really expressed and honored their culture. The Ho-Chunk still dance and occasionally open the ceremony to others, but they've moved their performances back into the spiritual realm of their lives now that they have an alternate way to make money. The Ho-Chunk, once called the Winnebago, are believed to be the first people to live on this land. Bennett took a picture of their Chief, Yellow Thunder, shortly before the Chief's death in 1883. Looking at the guidebook picture of the thin white-haired man, who looked more intense than frail, made me think of John Muir's description of an old Indian in the Sierra Nevada who "looked like an ancient tree-stump."

Yellow Thunder made amazing compromises to live in his land with the white settlers. In 1826, the government recognized that the land of southern Wisconsin was owned by the Winnebago—a meaningless act that did nothing to dissuade European settlers from claiming the land under the protection of governmental authorities. The Army tried to dispatch the natives away from their land in a forced foot journey in 1865, but many of the Ho-Chunk peacefully walked back to Wisconsin. Yellow Thunder, the leader, returned on foot from Nebraska at least four times to the home he called "Where wave and rock and tall pine meet." Half of the relocated tribe also returned, and eventually they were allowed to homestead and purchase their own land.

The three of us walked around the small caves and rock formations. Small golden birch leaves rained gently on our path and whispered against our faces and clothes. An occasional maple tree trumpeted crimson loudly enough to startle us into closer examination of the green skeletal hand hiding in the venation of each red leaf. Hemlocks held firmly to their verdant lace, offering a beautiful counterpoint of harmony. We walked in a line—DJ, I, and, Amber—all spread out far enough to experience individually the rays of sun shining in an azure sky and warming the ridge and our faces. Remember how this feels, I told myself, knowing it could be six or seven months before our northern sun offered this blessing again. Our trail traversed three quarters of the way up a rounded cliff and tapered when a wooden guardrail appeared at the top of the buff that faced the river.

We moved in, shoulder to shoulder, and looked out at the land and water of the Ho-Chunk. Branches of birch gilded our sunlit view of the wide bay of river and the surrounding State-owned natural areas. Pines topped the cliffs across the calm dark mirror of water. Creamy cliffs doubled their height in a trompe l'oeil of reflection. Each beauty was a resource for the spirit and the body. The woods on the cliffs have supported deer, bear, mink, quail, turkey, and more. Northern pike, walleye, perch, sturgeon, trout, and others still thrive in the fresh water. The wildlife and scenery brought tourist dollars just as the wildlife had brought substance to the Ho-Chunk of old. We imagined the primitive scene, white winters with the points of natives' tipis dotting the frozen river. Long before European settlers built shanties and dipped their poles into holes in the ice, Ho-Chunk would lie supine on thick hides under the shelter of their tipis and spear sturgeon swimming beneath their windows into the river. Settlements on the bluffs offered an advantage of high visibility over approaching enemies.

Just before we began our descent to the boat landing, I began to realize why the river was so wide and calm here. We'd passed a dam and power station in downtown Wisconsin Dells. This fat, lazy river was not the same as the rushing waters we'd seen in Bennett's pictures or imagined from a river that inspired the name Yellow Thunder. A portion of the bluffs and rock formations must be buried under this strangled river. I didn't tell the kids my theory, but I remembered that the Wisconsin is sometimes called the "hardest working river in the world" because it drops over 1,000 feet in just 430 miles, tempting civilization with its potential energy. The stunning view before us was tamed and diminished by a hydroelectric dam.

Back aboard, our guide confirmed for me that the dam had raised the river about seventeen feet. He pointed out that the channel markers here were initially placed when the river valley flooded after the 1908 dam was completed. Acres of trees in the path of the unnatural flood were buried alive; some were more than twenty feet tall. The skeletons of trees passively attacked the hulls of boats on the river until a channel was cleared by cutting off the tops of the trees. Even though most of the submerged forest must have rotted into sediment by now, boats play it safe by navigating in the channels of the truncated.

The dam increases the water pressure behind its bulk and forms a lake or widens a river while stealing land, blocking migration corridors, changing weather temperatures and oxygen levels, and fragmenting habitats. C.S. Lewis wrote in *The Abolition of Man*, "What we call Man's power over Nature turns out to be a power executed by some men over other men with Nature as its instrument." The dam trades resources for energy. I'm complicit in this trade: I do enjoy my electricity, and up to 10 percent of all Wisconsin's electric power comes from our dams.

When we again entered the shadow of the narrows, I thought about how turbulent the water must have been. I didn't complain to the kids about the unnatural calm and tried to focus on the staggering beauty that remained. Wildlife still flourished here. A raptor flew across the river calling a shrill "kak-ik-ik." DJ and I both pointed and he sputtered, "Bald eagle." Amber looked up, but the significance of our once-endangered national symbol didn't seem to register, and I was uneasy about every sight and experience turning into a lecture. Instead, we talked about lunch.

The memory of the giant lumberjack stayed with Amber, and when she asked about him, I agreed to take the kids to Paul Bunyan's cook shanty before our hike at Mirror Lake. We sat on benches in front of gingham-covered wooden slabs and tin and enameled dishes. The walls and shelves were covered with pioneer contrivances: yokes, axes, horseshoes, hoes, and old pictures. I waited for Amber's questions about the frontier doodads, but only one question came before the fried chicken. "Who's Paul Bunyan?"

After I explained the American folk tale based on "tall tales" and the fun the lumberjacks had in reaching new heights of extemporaneous invention, Amber recognized the nature of this game. "Oh, it's like when we talked about what went on in the bathroom."

She had it exactly right. The kids took the all-you-can-eat promise seriously, and both seemed disappointed they could only manage two pieces of cake for dessert. The brief drive to Mirror Lake still took enough time for them to feel the weight of their lunch settling in their eyelids. They asked to skip the hike. No mercy from me. We were only hiking a few miles, making a circle to the lake and Echo Rock, and if my old bones could make this easy walk, theirs could.

Mirror Lake isn't a natural lake. It's a flooded river valley formed in 1880 by a milldam. When this dam was built (as was true with most dams) developers didn't understand the concept of fish as migratory nor did they know that the stagnation of a river changes water temperature, sedimentation, and vegetation. Occasionally, the fish got lucky, and the dam didn't interfere with migrations. We didn't understand why ichthyic populations sometimes continued to thrive in the presence of a dam, and sometimes they didn't. Now that we know more, a greater responsibility accompanies each dam decision. Wisconsin is big on dams. Hydroelectric power dams originated in Appleton, Wisconsin in 1882 on the Fox River. The industrious immigrants were eager to exploit the resources of land and water. My ancestors did this, not understanding the trade they made and the sacrifices they forced on the ecosystem. A dam seemed to represent good old American ingenuity, human control over nature—an idea that no one questioned.

The lake captured the images of white cirrus clouds and the crowded bank of rich autumn colors. Dark tree trunks and the occasional white birch pillar gave the picture strong lines of composition indicative of bold artistry. I'd asked the kids to pick up the most interesting leaves they could find, which made them look at the ground. DJ spotted poison ivy and called Amber over to see the woodland hazard. October is late enough in the season to see the white berries, and when DJ taught her the saying, "Leaves of three, let it be. Berries white, run in fright," he took off running, and she followed screaming in jest. I hoped that on the next leg of the hike I might be able to get them to be quieter, as this region was known for a rich diversity in wildlife.

At the midpoint of our walk, we were on a road in a campground. I told them about the animals we might see if we were careful: deer, mink, beaver, raccoons, red fox, woodpeckers, and nuthatches. As we turned in to the Echo Rock Path, a young couple came toward us. One of them whispered, "There are three deer right around the bend."

Just then, Amber felt the descent in the path and let the momentum of the hill give her a running ride down the hill. Her rambunctious pace was most likely responsible for scaring away the deer.

DJ looked at me aghast. "Doesn't she know how to walk in the woods quietly?"

"I wasn't clear with her about how to act here, and she doesn't understand." Amber was enjoying herself.

My son, now tall enough to walk in step and rhythm with me, momentarily rested the side of his head against my shoulder. I gently shook him off before we came into view of Amber, concerned his action would make her feel like an outsider, and simultaneously concerned that I'd offended my son. The woods graciously distracted us.

The kids and I all searched the ground for the best leaves and in the process found brilliant red berries on the jack-in-the-pulpits and Indian pipes, also known as "ghosts of summer." These waxy white saprophytes of deep forest shade stand higher than the leaf litter of the forest floor. Natives tell of a legend that wherever people have quarreled, the pipes grow from the ground as a symbol of Nature wanting to make peace.

Our path was paved with yellow flecks of birch leaves, and it did seem as if the benevolent earth wanted to forgive. This area, mutilated and flooded by the dammed-up river was nevertheless a flourishing woodland. Since 1990, Wisconsin has removed fifty dams from rivers. Crumbling dams built in the 1930s, when the Tennessee Valley Authority spread dam-building fever across the nation, need expensive repairs. In the cost-benefit analysis, it's cheaper to remove them. Even in the city, the number of fish species in the Milwaukee River has increased from four to thirty-five due to dam removal. More and more frequently, city dwellers hang their poles from bridges and bring home dinner. We've learned that the former impoundments (artificial lakes and ponds) revegetate within one growing season following removal and we've learned that the increased recreational opportunities for fishing, canoeing, and wildlife watching on the free-flowing water create a tourism revenue source for the surrounding communities. Bennett had fought the hydroelectric dam at the Dells, understanding that the river valley's long-range economic value resided in its unique beauty. Others thought industry was more important. Toward the end of his life, he knew he lost his battle and watched the workers fell trees from the scenic bluffs as they began dam construction. Tourism now defines the economy of the Dells. Bennett's desire to protect the natural beauty of the area was economically wise. It seems by accident that the diminished beauty of the Dells is still grand enough to draw visitors.

Our path wound around a sandstone rock with a 100-foot diameter that jutted out to a peninsula in the lake. A silent parade of two canoes paddled into their reflection. Amber waved at the mother/son and father/daughter teams, and the dad in a red Wisconsin Badgers sweatshirt waved an exaggerated arch to us. I believe DJ could visualize himself in that canoe scene both as a son and a father. I don't know if Amber believed this park, lake, and forest were hers.

I asked her if she'd like to go canoeing sometime.

"I'm not a good swimmer."

"If I can find a place with calm water that is shallow enough to stand in, would you like to try?"

"Maybe when it's warmer, but next time I want to go bowling."

I agreed to the bowling and encouraged her to make a pact with me to canoe next summer. The canoe family gently towed their rippling V's further away from us.

DJ turned his attention to the thirty-foot-high Echo Rock and tried yelling into little caves in the sandstone, "I'm an idiot" and hearing no reply, created a mock echo response, "You're an idiot… You're an idiot."

Amber repeated the game into another mini-cave; the joke held up. The path led us back to our car, and I pulled a cooler from the trunk. The kids downed their juice before we hit the main highway and then immediately fell asleep. We traveled south past the ancient Baraboo range where the Nature Conservancy was racing with developers to buy land on these hills, which hold the largest block of upland forest in southern Wisconsin and some of the most ancient exposed rock on the earth. Signs directed me back to my Milwaukee while my navigator slept.

My city—that's how I think of Milwaukee, even though I've moved just beyond its edge. Those from a grander metropolis might think it quaint that I've stood on the Lake Park Bridge, looked at our Midwest skyline, and traced William Wordsworth's urban tribute from "Composed on a Westminster Bridge" in my mind:

> "Earth has not anything to show more fair.
> Dull would be he of soul who could pass by a sight
> so touching in its majesty."

I love Milwaukee's diversity—the parade of summer ethnic festivals, the Old World architecture, the eclectic arts scene. But poverty proliferates in the city, and the lines of racial segregation hold. I never imagined I'd be guilty of "white flight" and be one of those suburbanites who uses the resources of the city but spends her money and pays taxes in the suburbs. I did leave, after failed attempts to help my older daughter get a decent and safe education in the city schools. Andrea couldn't get into the best school because she didn't "enhance the racial balance." She showed me a book report decorated with big red A. When I looked closer, I noticed the report stopped mid-sentence. "Is there another page?" I asked.

"No." The teacher had asked for a full page, and once the requirement was met, my little scholar just put her pen down.

When her grades began to slip and included a D and an F on her report card, I asked for a meeting. The Vice Principal told me to ease up on my standards saying, "We praise the kids for a C average." That's when I gave up and moved to a smaller home only blocks from the city, but in a much better school district. And that is how I justify my abandonment.

The troubled part of Milwaukee has not seen improvement, while the city has built a new stadium for the Brewers baseball team, a river-walk corridor along the Milwaukee River, and facilitated a rash of upscale residential high-rises overlooking the rivers and Lake Michigan. The downtown flourishes where it can be exploited for financial gain, and it is a beautiful city. But, we neglect the land and the people in our poorest urban areas as if the people of the city, suburbs, and state wouldn't prosper with their renewal. When Jonathan Kozol writes about New York in *Amazing Grace*, the words ring true for Milwaukee and, I think, all cities. "The notion of ghetto as 'sin' committed by society is not confronted."

Just like those at the bottom of Amber's ramp, people have backed away from that which they saw as disagreeable, and they dragged along as many resources as they could carry. We've moved from the city to the previously unspoiled land of the suburbs, leaving behind the place and the people that we do not value. City dwellers do make a smaller imprint on the land than those who build sprawling homes in the suburbs. If we could turn around and face the problems of the city and make it a more desirable place to live, we might save our few remaining natural areas from further human domination and exploitation. The writer Scott Russell Sanders, in *Writing From the Center*, makes a sapient observation: "Those who follow us, and inherit from us a severely damaged world, will surely look back on our time and ask what we were doing while the earth burned."

Amber and her family didn't seem to be worrying about the earth's degradation; that's a concern generally fostered by those who are not fretting about how to juggle bills and survive. I wanted to make a difference for Amber. Maybe my motivation was to make myself feel better—to believe I made a bit of difference in her life. But no, that's not true; I wanted to make a big difference—to save her.

We turned east, and flocks of geese began to cross the highway—small trails of dots undulating high in the sky. Their V's shifted and honked in and out of sensory range. I pulled over at a wayside to watch them. Flocks of the Canada Goose are so common that I generally fail to stop and appreciate the long stretched neck and elegance of each bird and flock as they fill our landscape. In the 1930s, they were nearly extinct because of over hunting and habitat destruction, but people who cared worked with legislators and landowners, spent money, set aside land, and restored wetlands to save the Canada Goose. And they flourish in our imperfect landscape because people decided they were important enough to save.

When H.H. Bennett died, the vibrancy of his love for the Dells remained alive and potent in his family. His son-in-law, George Crandall, and his grandchildren spent their lives purchasing land along the Wisconsin River, including Witches Gulch. They worked together to restore native forests. The family transferred hundreds of acres of land to be held in a natural trust so visitors would be able to experience the beauty that had filled Bennett's life. Crandall's beliefs led him to care for the land and the people who would live long after his dust had blown down river. He said, "No man could ever own the Dells, just be its custodian for a while."

One child slept in the front seat, one in the back, both closer to adulthood than either of them realized. Trails of geese continued southward, and we crossed their route below, traveling eastward, back to the city. As dusk pushed the day behind us, I wondered if perhaps I'd been a two-dimensional do-gooder, thinking I could solve the problem of Amber as if she were a depository of the nation's ills. She wasn't a problem anymore than DJ was. They were just kids, wonderful kids. They both lived in a country where the growth in the poverty rate has often surpassed the nation's economic growth rate. I knew that soon both children would wake to adulthood and to the responsibilities and burdens we have left for them. The issues are enormous, but all I could think to do was to be Amber's friend.

STILL AUTUMN

"Just at the age 'twixt boy and youth,
when thought is speech, and speech is truth."
SIR WALTER SCOTT

When I was a child, my days were wild and unpredictable, and I sometimes miss the peaks of emotion present in that old life. Most of the time, I abhor the drama of my past when my life centered on the loudness of my hard-drinking parents. But that day in the still-young wilderness of the Schlitz Audubon Center with DJ, during our quiet moments, I wondered if the life we'd built for our last child—this last-chance-to-get-parenting-right son—held all the joy and excitement we wished for him. Was our life too quiet and too correct?

DJ is the "ours" in our *yours-mine-and-ours* family. Before marrying Paul, my nuclear family was only a duo—me and my daughter, Andrea. She was born into a marriage of two young kids who hadn't a clue about how to choose a spouse or build a life. My daughter grew up without her divorced dad and with a mother who was often at work, in college, or at home, studying. We did have our intense doses of scheduled together time, squeezed in between responsibilities while I strained to build a stable life and advance from nurse's aide to director of nursing. Paul's three children were more privileged than my Andrea, and they enjoyed the devotion of their stay-at-home mom, who grew to be dissatisfied with her often-absent physician husband. So now, here we are: Paul, with a history of giving most of his life to his job; Amy, practiced in allocating her time to the survival needs self-evident in single parenting and career building; and DJ, born to oh-so-responsible older parents.

DJ is eleven, and our other kids are all over twenty-five years old. My youngest camped and hiked with me since he was able to walk, and we grew accustomed to our outdoor time together while I served as his Cub Scout den leader. Conceived in a sleeping bag at Mauthe Lake, he's always seemed at ease in nature. He isn't, however, surrounded by riotous family fun. DJ's life has been subdued by the nature and age of his family. At many of our holiday celebrations, we draw our guest list from those who live near, at Luther Manor Retirement Center. Many of the adults at these geriatric festivals display their wildest party nature when they accept my coffee. They generally drink decaf, but I mix caffeinated beans and decaf to make my brew. Wow, what a night we had last Thanksgiving. Grandma stayed up until nine. DJ's always loved his older relatives, perhaps realizing that their overlapping life spans were narrow and therefore precious in their brief commonality. He collected jokes for them, gave cello and piano recitals, and listened to answers to his questions, which were only phonetically related to his original queries. And just like he has always been accommodating to the elder set, he's generally been good about our nature outings.

Even though DJ willingly accompanies me on our walks, he usually wants to know what else is in it for him. This time he settled for a stop at a bookstore and breakfast. Over George Webb Restaurant's pancakes, DJ kept kidding me about my literary fascination at the store. I'd leaned against a pillar and started to read Hannah Holmes' *The Secret Life of Dust: From the Cosmos to the Kitchen Counter, the Big Consequences of Little Things.* Suddenly hyper-aware of the concentration of dust between my eyes and the pages of the book, I'd read about the little particles we will all become and how many millions were floating in my morning orange juice. Realizations of the matrix in my environment, the tads of camel hair, particles of diamond dust, and some creepy minuscule monsters that drank my juice as I did, entranced me. DJ's chuckle drew me out of the book.

He'd been bending in front of me, reading the title. "You're reading about dust?"

"Yeah. It's amazing to consider that some of these particles," I pointed to a ray of low-November sun illuminating a concentration of specks in the air, "are flakes of skin supporting a village of microscopic life."

He took the book from my hand and returned it to the shelf. "Someone needs to stop you, Mom."

I could have held onto the book, picked it back up, or argued the point. Instead, I found myself mired in DJ's judgment of me. Reading a book about dust sounded so nerdy. I had to consider just how big of a geek I'd become.

Before we arrived at the Audubon Center, DJ joked about adding Holmes' book about dust to my Christmas wish list. While we drove past the wooded lots and symmetrically landscaped front entrances of the immense colonial homes of Bayside, DJ fired off his list of playful ammunition.

"You'll probably want your star calendar again so you can be sure to make us stand outside in the freezing night when the rings of Saturn and moons of Jupiter are visible in your telescope. Dad heard you telling Aunt Julie about the Walt Whitman poetry recording from the library that made you cry, so that CD might be on Dad's list for you. You want a mushroom identification book, and now probably a book on dust."

"Would you rather I asked for a leather miniskirt and Cuban cigars?" I didn't give him time to answer before I stepped out into the nearly miraculous warm November sun. With snow in the forecast for next week, this clear fifty-degree day felt like an unexpected last reprieve before the winter current would cover much of our landscape in a chilling sea of white.

Most of Wisconsin's undeveloped land teems with hunters in November, so we planned to walk in this protected sanctuary. The Schlitz Audubon Center harbors the largest stretch of undeveloped Lake Michigan shoreline in Milwaukee County, and it's here primarily because of an obstinate woman who wasn't even allowed to attend the male-only Board of Directors' meetings where the land use decisions were made. In 1885, the Joseph Schlitz Brewing Company purchased a tract of farmland nine miles from downtown Milwaukee on the shores of Lake Michigan as a place to rest their draft horses. By the 1950s, the Schlitz Foundation began to consider proposals for the Uihlein Nine-Mile Farm, including the popular option: high-rise luxury housing and a men-only golf course. Dorothy K. Vallier convinced her cousin, Joseph Uihlein—a Board member—that the land should be a nature sanctuary and proposed it be developed and managed under the auspices of the Audubon Society. She spent decades convincing the Shlitz men to continue to reapply to the Audubon powers, who kept turning them down because of the costs involved. For those twenty years, she worked from the outside, wielding her non-official influence in the community and on the Board to thwart lucrative development proposals. After Vallier secured the Audubon-required endowment (a large portion of which came from her personal account), the naturalized farmland became a National Audubon Education Center in 1974. Now in her late nineties, she's served on the Schlitz Audubon Center board for more than thirty-five years.

DJ listened to my adoration of Vallier, and I flattered myself guessing this birdwatcher must be a fellow geek. I'd given DJ a camera for this trip, and he was more interested in seeing the landscape through his new frame than listening to my stories. Oaks, birches, sumac, and more had dropped their autumn cover weeks ago and now rested in the spent leaves of summer. Parallel trunks disclosed their architectural scaffoldings of branches, some teardrop shaped, some round, and some in artistic free form but all impressive in the intricacies of their frameworks. DJ looked up the tower of a wide elm and studied the view in his frame. I imagined he envisioned the passage of time and recycled life that had been elevated to the open sky above the forest. When I asked him what he saw, he told me the two knots at the middle of tree looked like a lady's chest. When I looked up the trunk, I had to agree.

Between the arbor pillars, the blues of Lake Michigan blended into sky, obscuring the horizon. Ahead of us stood the observation tower. As we approached the structure, a family with a quintet of vociferous kids scooted around us and ascended the stairs. We followed.

Waiting one level below, while DJ climbed to the highest platform with the others, I looked out to the lake that had formed my sense of direction since I was a child. About 120 miles across the lake to Michigan and 300 miles from north to south, it fills the eyes' view as fully as any ocean. I always thought I was blessed with an innate internal compass because I could access an inner awareness of my orientation to the lake. Stargazing in a field in the nearby suburb, New Berlin, I had located north by first facing the lake, miles away and out of sight, toward the east, and then turning left.

The wind on the tower carried a brisk current of lake air, fresh but with a hint of fish smell. This was a smell from my childhood. When we lived in a flat on Milwaukee's east side, my dad would drive me to Bradford Beach with a six- or twelve-pack of beer in a cooler and one grape or orange soda for me cooling among his Pabst Blue Ribbons. And always in my memory, I see one amber bottle open and wedged between his thighs as he drove. He'd girl-watch while I played in the waves, not really swimming in the cold and strong undercurrent but teasing the lake by running just to the white hem at the water's edge as it came to greet me. I'd run away from the brisk advancement back to the warm sand. Eventually, Dad would offer me my soda; I'd never ask for it.

Dad's slicked back black hair, side burns, and crooked sneer gave him an Elvis-type persona. Girls smiled and talked about how cute I was as they flirted with him. He might pat my blonde curls as I sat with my legs in a circle and buried my sole-to-sole feet with little shovelfuls of sand. A cooler full of empty bottles would clink and thud as Dad and I walked back to the car, so he could get ready for his second-shift job.

Girls always looked at him. He'd strut so casually, smiling and relaxed. He might break into song and hug me or yell for me to "quit lagging behind and walk faster." Sometimes he called me useless; sometimes he called me "Peanut." I didn't know at four or five years old that he was drunk. I only knew that if I didn't fuss, I could go to the beach. Dad always drove sporty cars—Thunderbird, Mustang convertible, and GTO. I felt cool because he was cool. In winter (or even on a sunny autumn day like the day at Audubon), he'd sometimes take me to bars or to the local garage to "suck a few beers" with his buddies. They'd spend the early afternoon with their heads under the hood of some hot rod at Scotty's garage. Dad let me turn the handle on the red metal vending box and crank out a handful of salty peanuts. Garage patrons would walk by me and tell me I was a good girl for sitting so still. I knew the secrets to impressing adults: Don't ask for anything; don't touch anything; don't complain; don't spill. Any violation could lead to a spanking and certainly to being yelled at. Sitting and watching became my job, but I preferred my outdoor duties when birds, bugs, and plants kept me company. My quiet creed usually worked for me. My parents exacerbated the outrages in each other, and their fights could terminate in the emergency room or with dents kicked into the car or with one of them gone for a few days or weeks.

DJ appeared beside me from the upper level of the tower. "Why are you staying down here?"

"I prefer the calm. We'll have to be quiet and wait for a while to see if any of the birds show up again."

"Is that family bugging you?"

"I know five young kids have to be noisy, but I didn't come here to listen to people. I'll just be patient, and when they move on, we'll watch and listen for the birds."

A scramble of footsteps bounded and passed behind us. DJ elbowed my arm and nodded his head toward the upper platform. He led the way up the stairs, and I remembered being about twelve and coming out of the bathroom to see my dad pulling down the folding stairs to the attic and climbing them in his underwear and dress shirt. He'd been replacing an overhead light fixture in the front room, and I guessed he had some quick chore to finish in the attic. When the doorbell rang, I walked around the stairs to see my mom open the door to their friends, the two couples they were going out with to hear Jerry Lee Lewis, who was playing at The Annex nightclub. Mom wore high heels and a bright striped mini-dress. Her blond hair was short on her neck but ratted high and smoothed over. She served gimlets and rumacki that perfumed the house with the aroma of broiled bacon. When they asked about Dad, Mom said he was cleaning up. She said he'd been installing a new light, and she pointed to the ceiling as evidence. From a hole in the middle of the ceiling, Dad's head emerged clenching a light bulb in his teeth. They were all so jovial and quick to laugh. Just as they lamented that the fixture didn't work, the light in his mouth illuminated. Dad had screwed the bulb into an electrical socket with a switched cord that ran up the left side of his face, and mom had seated everyone to the right side of his head. He held the switch in one hand and waited for his cue to electrify the little crowd. By the second round of gimlets, my dad got his pants (I never knew why he didn't wear his pants to the attic) and quickly caught up with the cocktail count. The drinks seemed to make the story's retelling even more fun than the actual event. The lady friend explained her shock at seeing the human light, and she reached forward and pinched the rumacki, which I was forbidden to have unless there were leftovers. She held it in front of her face and finished laughing before she delicately nibbled and crossed the ankles of her white stiletto boots.

From the hall, I imagined myself drinking highballs, wearing white high-heeled boots with miniskirts, and kissing all my men-friends on the mouth like my pretty mom did. I'd grow to have beauty-parlor hair, eat rumacki, throw my head back, and laugh very loudly. I still have a square snapshot that shows Dad's smile and clenched teeth around the lit bulb. Most of the family pictures ended up at my home when my parents divorced and moved. DJ has seen all the pictures of my dad as light fixture and the stack of photos of his cars. Our Saturn and minivan don't have the same appeal as my dad's '57 T-bird with the porthole top. He loved to take the T-bird out on sunny days without the hardtop. He said he had to "clean out the engine" and drove pedal to the metal. He took me along even before he had found a restored passenger seat. A wooden crate of empty Glenn Rock Soda bottles served as my seat. I pretended to enjoy the rattling car and bottles and the feeling of being in a clanking tornado. The wind made whips of my curls, erratically beating the cheeks and eyes of my chubby round face. My fear squelched forever in me the enjoyment of speed that others find in motorcycles and downhill skiing. I always went for a drive with Dad whenever he asked. I wanted to be cool, even if it killed me—because I loved him, and because he wanted to be with me.

On the top of the tower, DJ and I faced the wind coming from the east, and my hair blew straight back behind my head. From this vantage point, the landscape expanded, and blue filled the immense dome of sky.

About a half-mile south, five children and two adults appeared to vibrate slowly, lots of movement and a little forward advancement, like colorfully dressed ants on a winding trail. A pair of cardinals low in bushes attracted DJ's attention. The coming winter had already sent most of our colorful birds adrift. The orioles, tanagers, towhees, iridescent indigo buntings, and ruby throated hummingbirds all took their exotic plumage back to the tropics. The stunning red of the cardinal offered a comforting reminder that all that is bright and beautiful had not abandoned those of us who dwell in northern winters. Wind muffled most of the birdcalls, but a loud "churrr" call with rolling R's turned our heads to a male red-bellied woodpecker. Over nine inches long, it's the largest woodpecker generally seen in Milwaukee County. DJ knows this beauty with a zebra back and wide red stripe from forehead to nape. When one first came to our home feeder, its size startled me. Longer than the suet cage, she (a red stripe originated at the back of her head rather than from her forehead) contorted herself around the feeder, which was too short for her to perch on and eat while uncurled. My first red-bellied in my own back yard brought me joy in the novelty of its size and distinctive coloring, as if it were almost too wild to be seen at a feeder in a hand-laid rock garden. The same joy overcomes me every time I see one.

Standing in the corner of the tower, DJ leaned against me so that even though we were alone on the tower, we took up very little space. He rolled around me, semi-circling from a bit behind me to a bit in front of me, all the while keeping in shoulder-to-shoulder contact. We spotted black-capped chickadees and gold finches. They had put away their bright yellow plumage for their coats of brown, which the experienced birder sees as a dull olive green.

Startled by a flurry of winged activity, our eyes flitted from trees to ground to bushes. There were at least fifty birds, but what were they? I made my eyes focus on just one, and then the Wordsworth lines came with recognition, "Art thou the bird whom Man loves best, The pious bird with the scarlet breast?" They must have been migrating in a flock. Our official State Bird, yet I'd never seen a flock this large. Busy and bossy, the robins chased each other, establishing dominance for prime resting and eating areas. Most settled in an open area behind the tower, so we turned our backs to the lake and watched them forage and compete for choice limbs on a crabapple tree. These thrushes migrate together and disperse once they reach their destination. Our last robins of the season, we didn't expect to see more until early spring when they would return to feed on the shriveled rose hips of all the bushes that are not tended by overzealous pruners.

DJ asked, "What's the big deal about robins? A bunch of states use them as State Birds, and everybody makes a big deal when they come back in spring. Other birds come back too."

"I think it's the songs, DJ. Robins sing our spring songs for us. Their territorial songs are loud, recurrent, and happy. They sound like spring."

"You mean they sing for you?"

"Yes."

"Well, I'm truly grateful for robins if they sing instead of you."

We left the tower with DJ spitting over the railing at each turn of the stairs as he tested the wind. He wasn't afraid to spit into the wind, and this time the wind didn't return his fire.

I wanted to find the blooming witch hazel tree and bittersweet vine, which both flaunt their vivid blooms into December, so we pushed on to the woods, prairies, and ponds away from the lake. DJ kept his camera out and pointed it in all directions in a combination of adolescent energy and curiosity. I tended to look where he pointed the camera.

At first glance, the woods looked brown and monochromatic, but when we looked closer, the colors transformed to more intense and varied shades. At the base of a dead stump, turkey tail fungus grew loud seasonal decorations. Looking close at the six-inch fans of striped color, we saw shades a kindergartener might choose to decorate his gobbler picture. Arches of tan, brown, orange, and purple layered and repeated themselves in beautiful redundancy. One clump held twenty-one half-disks of colors, and there were more clumps deeper into the woods where we would not walk. We felt as if we had been invited to walk the trail by Mrs. Vallier and were proper guests. The word "fungus" bears the stigma of something slimy, but these beauties felt like fine worn leather.

Tall red cedars hugged our trail and scented the air with a richness that fell just short of sweet. I stopped to feel the rippled texture of their fibrous bark and admired the red and tan in matching hues. Verdant leaves of flattened and blunted needles flaunted their adornments of shiny blue berries in contrast to the absence of deciduous color.

At the prairie, tall stalks of thistle dotted the grasses with deep black seed heads. Forty-foot-wide stands of red dogwood posed in flashy clusters before a wide ridge of tanned and dried miscanthus grass that waved and rustled in the cooling afternoon wind. Our trail wandered near ponds of ducks and geese that seemed to be settling in for the winter as they sauntered in the still water with an occasional push of their webbed feet toward the slowly moving shadow-line that separated day from evening and shrunk the sunshine of their afternoon. If they were migrators, they'd have been busy eating and stockpiling energy for the flight ahead.

Woodlands and prairie fields alternated dominance, and after a few miles, DJ put away his camera and started to play with my arm. Whacking the back of my elbow, he'd send the arm swinging forward, then bat it back and slap it forward again in a soft rhythm that didn't really hurt. He didn't have to say the words; I knew he was thinking, How much farther?

"It's less than two miles back." There was a shorter route back, but I still wanted to see the blooms of the witch hazel and bittersweet, and I felt no need to bring up the option of the quarter-mile path to the parking lot.

I might have made a mistake; he seemed to have met his nature quota for the day. He kept swinging my arm and started to sing, "Lucy met the train. The train met Lucy. The tracks were juicy. The juice was Lucy." He finished that number and went into long rendition about a pirate mutilation. "Being a pirate is all fun and games, till somebody loses an eye. It spurts and it squirts and it jolly well hurts; you can't let your mates see you cry.…"

And before long, I sang with him, "Being a pirate is all fun and games, till somebody loses an ear. It drips down your neck, and it falls on the deck.…"

We probably walked right past the witch hazel, chugging our arms and marching in rhythm. We never did find the spidery yellow blooms on a small understory tree that I'd heard bloomed in the area. As we crossed a paved service road, I saw a couple standing still in a meadow in front of us. I grabbed DJ's arm and pulled on his wrist like you'd pull on a light chain to turn it off. He was quiet. I pointed ahead. "Those people are very still. They must see something."

We walked softly into the meadow, and the man, still thirty feet ahead of us, hyper-extended his wrist and showed us his palm. We stopped. He pointed into some brush on our right. A huge doe ate, chomping and sliding her lower jaw laterally and twitching her ears. She saw us, and we stood as statues. The man pointed again to the brush, and as we followed his hand signals and froze, an immense buck turned his head to us, displaying a shiny twelve-point rack. This buck had rubbed every bit of velvet off his antlers to look his best in preparation for the rut. Autumn is the season of love for deer; they pair up and mate when the male is most impressive. His brown shiny eyes watched over his seasonal sweetheart while she continued to eat. They were only about ten feet away but stayed as if they knew this was a no-hunting area. It's a rare treat to see a couple in love like this. After coupling, the male stays around only a few days to make sure no other male mates with his dear; then he leaves. Either of those deer could have bounded off at thirty miles an hour, but the female just moseyed away when she'd had her fill of dogwood, and the buck followed, always watchful and never lowering his head to eat.

DJ's words tenderly entered the quiet space. "He looked like he loved her."

"Yes, but doesn't it seem harsh that he leaves her so quickly?"

"Um, you want to talk harsh? What about the poor guy who's a black widow or praying mantis."

We both recalled a television show about the *Mantis religiosa*. The narrator had assured us that the religiosa was the only mantis consistently cannibalistic during mating. After dancing around each other and turning their thoraxes into graceful undulating S's, the male hopped up onto her back. While he continued his dance of love in rhythmic thrusts, the larger female turned her head toward the camera as if she were an exhibitionist and wanted to be sure we were watching. The mantis is the only insect that has an elongated thorax that looks like a neck and turns its head from side to side like a human. She continued turning her face upward to meet the trancelike gaze of her mate. We knew what was coming, but couldn't look away while she took three bites of his head. And while she chomped off his entire face and chewed, his abdomen continued to thrust. The voice-over told us, "In the religiosa species, head removal is necessary for ejaculation."

We reclaimed our feelings of tenderness for the short-lived romance of the deer and continued our walk. DJ drifted ahead of me. Dried compass plants whose leaves looked like over-cooked potato chips bent erratically as a band of purple finches poked at the black seed heads of a plant that had once been a favorite of the buffalo. The reeds of the dry grasses played their wind music as we finished our walk as audience to the symphony. DJ swung his arms dramatically and walked ahead of me as we each found our own thoughts.

I had learned to be taciturn in my childhood home for reasons that no longer existed. As a little girl, I waited for the time I could be noisy and wild and fun whenever I wanted, and by the time I was a young teenager, I joined in at my parents' parties. Older men noticed me, offered me drinks, and danced with me. Some started kissing me hello and goodbye, just as they did my mother. My parents were non-reactive to these events. Dad never taught me to dance, but a friend of his did, with his tub of scotch on the rocks gripped in his hand and clinking behind my back as we turned. Once I was attractive to these men, I was included in the parties. I soon discovered I didn't care to be around these adults, as their sophistication dissolved and their vowels slurred. As a small child, I did want to be part of my parents' fun, but by my late teens, I found reasons to avoid the parties that had started to feel creepy. As an adult, I realized more specifically that the danger of sexual abuse hovered around me at these parties, but at the time I don't think I was cognizant of the danger. I did find out that the drunks who didn't get loud got boring and could corner me and prey on my respect-your-elders attention while offering me their incoherent and unwelcomed philosophies. I took a lot of walks so as to spend as much time as possible away from the sloshy tumult in our home. In my early adulthood, I made my own turbulence that left me a single parent without an education, but I worked my way out and built a new life. My adult interests in astronomy, gardening, reading, birding, and nature were enhanced by the gift my parents gave me as a small child. They taught me to sit upon my throne of silence and learn the comfort and wonders found in stillness.

The cooling air inched winter closer with every step in our walk. Perhaps we would return in the season of snow, when the witch hazel seedpods burst and crack like a gun, a trait that changes the name of this tree in winter to snapping hazel. The lake, visible through the trees, would soon begin its winter art project of making ice sculptures with rolling waves. I tried not to lament the passing season and the expected bitterness of winter weather. Robert Frost loved his Vermont winters, yet he understood the melancholy I felt, as he expressed in the last stanza of "Reluctance."

> "Ah, when to the heart of man
> Was it ever less than a treason
> To go with the drift of things,
> To yield with a grace to reason,
> And bow and accept the end
> Of a love or a season?"

I will probably spend some winter evenings reading about dust, history, nature, and fictional lives, but I won't wear a miniskirt or white stiletto boots. Rather than watch me from the hall, DJ will lie on the sofa near my chair and read his new favorite author, Kristin Frankline. Occasionally, we'll interrupt each other to share a well-crafted line, a fascinating fact, or a joke. I could make rumacki. Paul and I can share the moniker of geek if that means we are quiet more than riotous. DJ can be the cool one in our home and keep us somewhat current on the new song releases from Atmosphere and Pert' Near Sandstone. We will host or attend a few parties, laugh and be silly, and occasionally be a bit loud, but we won't live the drama that I experienced as a child. I'd forgotten that I'd made that choice decades ago and again sixteen years ago when I chose to be with my contemplative Paul. This was the only authentic life I had to share with my son.

DJ, still twenty yards in front of me, turned around to face me. "Parking lot's just ahead." I nodded and watched his lanky limbs and broad strides carry him away. Only this spring he'd been in grade school when his voice sounded more like mine than his father's. His shoulders have grown broader than his hips, and his little love handles just above his belt melted away during his first football season. His growth during the year has been relentless in its message: There is so little of his childhood left.

The grassy path smoothed and widened just before the parking lot, and DJ performed a sloppy cartwheel ending with a distinctive thud on the blacktop. He never turned around to see if I was watching; he knew. Walt Whitman's words from "Song of the Open Road" appeared in my mind.

> "Now I see the secret of the making of the best persons.
> It is to grow in the open air and to eat and sleep with the earth."

DJ and I stood at each side of the car, doors open, drinking water and lingering in the day's final rays of sunshine. We'd walked quickly that last mile, and our bodies were warmed from within. We threw our sweatshirts in the backseat of the car to enjoy the brisk air. A pickup truck pulled in next to us, and DJ turned to close his car door to make more room in the adjacent parking spot. When he faced the woman in the truck, she smiled and gave him the okay sign. DJ pointed to his shirt that said, "Stop Reading My T-shirt" and nodded back to the good-natured driver, who was quickly off for her walk before the sanctuary closed.

Just before I lifted a foot to enter the car and end our autumn, I saw a burst of color ahead. Directly in front of our parking space, a bittersweet vine glowed in colors of fuchsia and orange. Tiny beacons of seedpods, hundreds of them, blazed bright in front of us. DJ followed me to the vine, and we studied the red arils, little fleshy fruits, and the orange capsules that fold back like petals, so bright they're almost garish in their celebration of themselves.

We stood silently, each inspecting the beautiful intricacy of the pods, smaller than a pea, but so sumptuous in their beauty it took us several minutes to ingest the diminutive wonders. They seemed almost too fancy for bird food, but then they were also the ripe fruit of sexual reproduction. In those moments of stillness, we seemed especially open to the revelations nature might have for us. I watched DJ inspecting the capsules and wondered if when he's grown he'll remember this day, the blue of the lake, the flurry of robins we watched from the tower, the hike, the deer, the silly songs, and the very end of a season. And I wondered if when he recognizes this seedpod in autumns of his future, he will remember the quiet moment with me when he first met the bittersweet vine.

EAGLE WATCHING

*"The peace I am thinking of is the dance of an open mind
when it engages another equally open one."*
TONI MORRISON

The driving distance from Wisconsin's east to its west coast is approximately the same as the distance between Salzburg, Austria and Prague in the Czech Republic. I suspect that most people who consider Wisconsin think of it as a land united from border to border by its identifying cartographic markers: cheese, farms, football, and beer. And I must admit, for many of the rural portions of the state, the cultural stereotype seems rooted in a superficial reality. The land, however, doesn't contemplate national or interstate borders or cultural stereotypes as it jolts and cajoles the elements of earth, creating and recreating the features of our natural world. For my son DJ and me, this west edge of the state was unfamiliar (if not exotic), and even though we didn't cross border and checkpoint, we did travel about 200 miles to the area of the state that is influenced not by our familiar Lake Michigan but by the Mississippi River. Last winter's visitors and residents near the river savored the sight of over 100 bald eagles gathering en masse near and on the great waters. In winter, the raptors migrate down the frozen Mississippi to open waters near the riverine convergences and churning dams that allow the raptors continuous brumal access to the open waters and to the fish. We wanted to see the symbol of our United States en masse. I wanted to experience assuredness that eagles lived in abundance in the Midwest, that they and their habitats were safe.

Once we passed Madison on our westward journey, I pointed over the dashboard to the changing landscape. "See how different the land is here." Glaciers had encircled the southwest part of the state but never covered this region. My son listened to his iPod. DJ's dark blue eyes under newly bushy brows scanned the landscape while his head bobbed to the music, and its rhythm momentarily changed to a nod. I had some expectation that the land would smooth out completely in the absence of the kettles and drumlins we'd passed on the way to Madison, because this region was called "the driftless area." We'd crossed one of the largest drumlin swarms in the world. At any other time of the year, it would have been easy to drive the land and not notice that the hills formed the shapes of teardrops. On this late December day, the departed leaves and frost-withered shrubs and grasses exposed the structure of the terrain, and a light sifting of snow settled into ridges and hollows, which further outlined the features as if by white chalk. The pointed end of the tear-shaped mound aimed in the direction of glacial advance while the rounded bluff-like end held the form the ice had given the land during the last advancing thrust of power and final retreat.

The land never did flatten to match my distant memory of driving this road to Prairie du Chien. This driftless land west of Madison lacked the kettles we knew from glaciated areas in the rest of the state, where huge chunks of buried ice melted and lowered the land as though on a slow one-way elevator, leaving deep hollows. West of Madison, V-shaped valleys divided gently rounded expanses of farmland. Ancient mountains had once risen out of a sea, but time had softy worn them into hills. A matrix of temporary rivers subsequent to the massive glacial melting had etched diminutive, yet distinct valleys between mounds.

I tapped DJ on the leg, and he pulled one side of his headphone off his ear. "Can you turn that off now? Watch for wildlife; I thought I saw a huge bird."

He complied, looked up and around, and in a deadpan voice announced and pointed to the wildlife and livestock around us. "Crow.

Cows. Hawk. Cows. Sheep. Horse. Cows." When he pointed up and simply declared "Bald eagle," he did not change the cadence of his monotone delivery. I pulled over and quickly swung open the car doors and stood resting my elbows on the roof and aiming my binoculars toward the soaring bird. A thick, dark body contrasted a stark white head and tail. Long, sturdy wings terminated in fingerlike wingtips that pointed back so the anterior edge of the wing formed an oblique angle. This raptor was gliding and steering on currents of air by tiny imperceptible movements, including individual control of the ten primary wingtip feathers. When eagles soar on rising currents to gain altitude, they stretch their wings wide with an entirely horizontal spread.

DJ never got out of the car, as I expected. He only turned his head to watch out the window, displaying only the mildest of interest.

I asked him if he was saving his excitement for the groups of eagles we expected to see at the Mississippi.

He shrugged. "There won't be as many as we saw in Alaska."

"You know, when I was a kid, I didn't see *any* eagles in Wisconsin." Indeed, by 1950, almost a decade before I was born, bald eagles didn't live in the lower two-thirds of the state. Efforts to save them didn't become serious until the seventies, when they were placed on the Wisconsin Endangered Species List. The first bald eagle I ever saw lived in a zoo and had only one wing. DJ, his dad, and I had seen hundreds of what looked like golf balls dotting trees on the Chilkat River near Haines, Alaska while on a trip to visit family. These white orbs were the heads of the mature raptors poised in the trees. We'd seen several swoop and plunge, hanging their feet into the river. Several had pulled fifteen- to twenty-pound salmon out of dark waters in what appeared to be a magic trick. But eagles thrived in this remote land primarily because Alaska's human population was too sparse to destroy the ecosystem. These bird populations are recovering in Wisconsin and in much of the continental United States largely because we stopped using DDT and tried to find a way to coexist with the only type of eagle that is specific to North America.

Bald Eagles are our national emblem; perhaps that's what really saved them. Our country would have looked pretty stupid had we killed off a species and symbol we supposedly revere. So, eagles have also become a symbol of ecological devastation and reclamation. While still threatened and in need of protection, they are no longer considered endangered.

DJ was unimpressed and unusually sullen, but he did continue his reportage for the rest of the trip to Cassville. "Horse. Cows. Eagle. Cows. Crow. Hawk."

I didn't stop him. We didn't stop for other eagles either, assuming we'd see many more. At least my son was looking, noticing. The spray of blemishes across his forehead reminded me that his feelings and moods about everything, including our trips, may have become more complicated in recent months, but he still came with me. If his running commentary was all he had to offer, I took it, happily.

For the last few miles DJ had been saying, "Cow, cow, cow." And goodness, there were a lot of cows. The view: gray skies, a few strips of leafless forest, barns, silos, and cows that wandered fenced swells of land deeply dissected with valleys. Several farmhouses hung Green Bay Packer flags from their front porches. Every edge and every depression in the landscape were outlined in white snow. We descended through patches of forests and steep bluffs that terraced out at the river town of Cassville, where we hoped to see more eagles or at least find the sites where they would congregate the next morning.

When I found the gazebo observation deck next to a closed-for-the-season Mississippi ferry landing, I invited DJ to come with me. He sat silently, and I walked away to the deck. At nearly three p.m., prime time for raptor viewing had passed, but I focused my binoculars to a spot about a half mile across a frozen river, close to a patch of open water and scanned the trees for golf balls. DJ appeared next to me with his binoculars. We spotted two large nests in the high branches of a white pine. DJ pointed to a tall elm with a similar broad nest, a thick disk of sticks. This nest must have been well-established, with a pair of experienced parents adding to the nest every year so that now it looked big enough for both of us to sit in. One golf ball did appear, and through the binoculars, we saw the mature bald eagle; by its huge size we guessed it was a female. This brawny mature bald eagle sat perched in her tree—and that was it, just one. Over 600 eagles were counted in this river area last winter; a few times, hundreds congregated at this very spot. Building my optimism on last year's count, I held on to my cocky confidence that'd we'd experience many more eagles the following morning.

Choosing a hotel with a pool did little to unveil the son I often called "Nutball." DJ watched a movie in the room while I planned the sites of the next morning's eagle watch. We played a tame game of Nerf football in the pool, ordered pizza, and set our alarm for an early sunrise.

DJ didn't eat a doughnut from the free breakfast buffet, even though a chocolate-covered custard-filled beauty sat on the top of the pile; he ate yogurt and an English muffin. He seemed to be needling me with his sullen maturity. I picked at my eggs, hoping he wouldn't notice I'd set the alarm way too early for the seven-thirty sunrise. Instead of complaining about my leisurely cup of coffee and time with the morning paper, he took a section and then said, "Mom, I heard you on the phone upset about Mr. Ehrlich. What did he do?"

For the previous few weeks, our local newspaper's editorial page and the neighborhood gossip had focused on a rift in community opinion. When a high school forensics team chose to perform a Jim Grimsley play, "A Bird of Prey," some parents strongly objected to its gritty subject matter: pedophilia, drug use, murder, and suicide. They also objected to profane language in the play. I explained to DJ that our neighbor, Mr. Ehrlich, wrote a letter of objection in which he called the play "filth" and obtained seventeen other signatures of concurrence. When our neighborhood protestor asked my opinion, and probably expected my support, I told him, in cautiously worded discussion, I thought difficult subjects should be addressed by high school students on the verge of adulthood and that plays with literary merit can be a vehicle to open essential dialogue. I asked him to tell me not about the content but about the message of the play. I knew that Grimsley was an award-winning novelist and playwright and that the students had won several awards for their performance as they advanced through local, regional, and state competitions. My first instinct about the play was positive, but I didn't have enough information to be sure.

News of my opinion had spread across the community, and I was fending off phone calls about my tolerance for the play and my objection to the school Superintendent's decision that the play couldn't be performed in school. When the students found a venue for the play in a Milwaukee theater, my husband Paul and I attended. The plot and characterizations showed the dark world that many teenagers face. The play was intense, but we thought it curious that the community would want to shield high school juniors and seniors from reality.

I talked to DJ about the importance of freedom of expression, the politically conservative climate since the September 11 terrorist attacks, and the polarization of liberal and conservative views that intensified after the initial blush of patriotic unity. I told him that by the time he was in high school, it would be time to consider these important issues. I also told him that the arts are supposed to shake things up, to make us think, to bring issues that must be dealt with out of dark shadows. I hoped my son understood. He seemed to.

Across the street from our hotel, a flock of ducks filled the open water of a rivulet. Every duck seemed to have something to quack about, so we went over to look—guessing they would be mallards. The frosted grass crunched under out feet, and even though we knew the grass was brown, the snow was white, and the trees trunks were dark brown, everything appeared in shades of grainy gray in the morning-weak light. The sound of what seemed to be a squeak toy clearly squealed amidst the quacks. Yes, there were over fifty handsome mallards, but somewhere in this undulating mass of green and brown heads, I hoped to find the curiosity I heard.

When my head stayed still and I smiled, DJ asked, "Watcha got?"

"Wood ducks, I thought I recognized that squeak."

If Steve McQueen were to be reincarnated as a duck, I think he would be a wood duck. They are so cool. I'd probably only seen about ten of these in my life, even though they are reported as common in the state. DJ couldn't remember the previous time we had seen them. These are the only ducks in North America who perch in trees. Only occasionally do they winter in the warmer southern parts of the state; generally, they migrate further south. The male wood duck is unique. Even his bill has three colors–black, white, and red. In summer, as preparation for catching the pseudo-bespectacled eye of a female, iridescent green and purple head feathers form a crest that sweeps down to his back. The male before us didn't wear his sexy pick-up clothes, but his more reserved crest and toned-down winter plumage. Two brownish females lingered toward the back of the flock, appearing aloof. Their tear-shaped white eye rings hugged their faces as if they wore the latest in European sunglasses. At one time, they were nearly extirpated from Wisconsin because they nest in mature trees coveted by loggers. When a female can't find her own nest in the hollow of a tree or duck box, or maybe when she's not in the mood or health for raising ducklings, she'll drop her eggs in the nest of another wood duck. These beauties usually live for less than two years, so the forfeiture of her eggs to another may be the loss of her only chance at rearing young. Watching them for a few moments was a gift, and when the male flew away, we also left.

The Mississippi surprised us as we drove Highway 18 to Iowa. Not just one river ran below the series of bridges we crossed, but multiple streams of ice streaked between large strips of woodland, which were actually islands in the frozen waters. Since the 1930s, when a series of locks and dams and gouged navigation channels transformed this land and river, the waters have run in braided streams with narrow cuts and channels that snake between islands of dense floodplain forest.

Iowa welcomed us by sign and directed us to Pike's Peak. DJ looked confused. "Pike's Peak is in Iowa? I thought it was out west."

"You'll find out in a little while," I said, expecting to hear his "Come on—tell me," but it didn't come. My teasing and withholding backfired in his silence.

A steep Iowa winding country road led us from farm to woodland. Perched high on the bluffs of the Mississippi, Pike's Peak State Park in Iowa offered a perspective of Wisconsin and the Mississippi that we terrestrial-bound creatures couldn't see without stepping outside the Dairy State. We headed straight for the view, fortunate that the thirty-degree day didn't carry much of a bite. We stood on a Paleozoic-age dolomite rock bluff with a 500-million-year history. Hundreds of feet below, the Wisconsin River flowed into the Mississippi's swirls of land and water. Islands—hundreds of them in C and S shapes, ovals, and some with their own interior lakes—wove through currents and created a striking fusion of earth and ice. This was the place where Marquette and Joliet first saw the Upper Mississippi River Valley in 1673. The area's indigenous inhabitants sculpted animal-shaped effigy mounds of dirt from 800 to 1200 CE. Not much is known about this native woodland culture because they didn't leave many signs of how they lived. This bluff was also the spot that impressed Lieutenant Zebulon Pike in 1805, when the government sent him here after the Louisiana Purchase to select a site for a military post. The post was eventually built across the river in Prairie du Chien, and Pike's name became associated with a discovery he made in Colorado several years later—the nation's second Pike's Peak. Park signs bragged that the land in this area was never developed, so it looked much as it had during the time of the effigy mound builders, but the land we saw was void of elk, buffalo, black bear, lynx, bobcat, marten, quail, wolf, prairie chicken, whooping crane, and, most sadly, the passenger pigeon—eliminated not only from this area but wiped from existence in every corner of the earth.

Our panoramic view made it easy to understand why this river valley and surrounding land with its scored dendritic patterns was well loved. Will Dilg, a bass fisherman, couldn't bear the thought of developers' plans to drain and dike the backwaters of this river valley. Dilg and fifty of his Chicago fishing buddies formed the Izaak Walton League in 1922. Two years later, they convinced Congress to form the Upper Mississippi River National Wildlife and Fish Refuge. This refuge crosses four states and six Congressional districts encompassing about seventy cities and towns. To accomplish anything at all in this refuge, competing interests have to put the needs of the refuge above their individual and economic interests. The Upper Mississippi, with its natural shoreline and abundant wildlife, flourishes in many ways, but the management is complicated, and natural losses seem at least as common as natural gains.

DJ studied the underside colors and flight of a raptor overhead. He identified the patterns in the *Peterson's Guide*. The rough-legged hawk was a first sighting for both of us. This buteo hovered higher than the bluff on broad wings which beat with the bravado of a muscle-flexing body builder. This tough guy wintered in our relative Midwestern warmth after having flown down from the arctic. The pebbled brown and cream body and wings with sprays of white feathers tipped in black looked as if he had carried bits of the rock-studded snowy tundra down here with him. He lifted his wings to make a wide V and turned right to the farmlands and their mice and moles.

No eagles. Not one.

I was pleased about seeing our first rough-legged hawk and thanked DJ for his identification. I'd subtly checked the book too; he was right. Winter bird watching in the Midwest doesn't yield the flourish of species we see during migration or breeding season. The islands and valley below had filled in the milder seasons with great blue herons, double-crested cormorants, and great egrets, up to 160 species of songbirds, tundra swans, and even white pelicans.

Our morning was still fresh, and we had other places to find our eagles. I led my quiet DJ back to the car and finally succumbed to my concern. "Is something bothering you, hon'?"

Shrugged shoulders told me he wasn't angst-free. His shrug was an I'm-not-quite-ready-to-talk response. I didn't have to push, though, not with a hike on the bluffs of Cassville ahead of us.

The sun had been up only about an hour, and the ice fishers were still setting up on the sloughs as we drove back over the plait of channels and island marshes. DJ strained to watch, ratcheting his head from fishing hole to fishing hole, looking for some action. Anglers here fish year-round, catching walleye, northern pike, bass, sauger, perch, crappies, sunfish, and catfish, but many of the species in this water are threatened. Dams obstruct breeding ranges and migration routes of some of the endangered fish, and invasive species such as Asian carp, accidentally released from fish farms on the lower Mississippi, contribute to the approximately forty types of fish listed as "threatened" or "of concern" by the State of Wisconsin.

Before the glaciers invaded, ancient fish prowled the waters of Wisconsin. With each glacial retreat, a few species migrated back to new and reformed rivers and lakes. These ancients don't disappoint in terms of how I imagine prehistoric fish might have looked. The paddlefish swims like a gray shark in the waters of the deep channels as they have done since fifty million years before the first dinosaurs. Its long nose comprises one-third of the length of its body and gives this toothless fish a fearsome saw tooth shark-type appearance. It swims with an open mouth and skims scads of tiny lives from the water while growing up to weigh nearly 200 pounds. Another huge and ancient fish, the sturgeon, browses along the river bottom. At up to 300 pounds, this giant, like the paddlefish, grows not on a skeleton but on a scaffolding of cartilage, much like the shark. Bony studded plates, similar to those that covered the ankylosaurs, line up in rows for exterior body protection. Four fleshy feelers drag the riverbed for snails, crayfish, worms, and insect larvae. DJ and I discussed how we could understand the excitement sport fishers felt when catching these stunning fish but wondered why anyone would keep the endangered fish once they knew that the female requires more than twenty years to mature, and even then, it spawns only every four to six years during its fifty-year lifespan. While the ancient exotic species are protected on the refuge, they migrate to rivers and streams where they are vulnerable to fishers who are guided by regulations that allow their harvest even before they reach the size and age at which they can reproduce.

DJ leaned to the window. He showed me only the back of his head, but I tried to engage him by capitalizing on his interest in the fish. "Would you like to come back and go ice fishing sometime?" I tried to tempt him with details of a potential winter trip: 134 species of fish here, borrowing Aunt Lil's ice shanty, bringing along chocolate brownies.

DJ began to flip through the radio channels. "No. I'd rather fish in summer."

He never found a suitable station while we traveled out of Prairie du Chien. Soon every hill brought us to cows: cows scattered from a herd and cows staggered in a far field and cows smattered over the crest of a steep hill. A line of black cows stood in the middle of the field in an orderly queue. DJ thought we caught them forming a conga line. When two cows were lying down, we imagined they were hiding ribbons on sticks they'd been swirling during their rhythmic gymnastic dancing routines. Two Holsteins standing head-to-head had been discussing how to finance skydiving lessons before we drove by the front of their pasture, and they tried to fool us with their empty expressions.

By the time we reached our hiking grounds just outside of Cassville, DJ was again quiet. Stone walls that once marked agricultural fields, previously owned by the state's first governor, slumped in long piles throughout the edges of the hardwood forest. We drove to the bluffs of Nelson Dewey State Park and chose a trail that snaked up and down a 400-foot bluff on the Mississippi. The river had reconfigured since Prairie du Chien and was now one flowing body of ice. Rocky bluffs settled into terraces, which supported tall prairie plants that had left their grasses and flowers in a dried arrangement. Some of the white asters still looked like diminutive daisies, their pious beauty and color preserved. Clusters of black-eyed Susan seed heads and thistles created dark polka dots floating above the golden stalks. Grasses swished in the dry wind. We walked over weathered limestone void of the scratches we were accustomed to seeing on bluffs where glacial sheets had dragged imbedded rocks over hard stones and gouged traces of their movement into the terrain. Old crumbling limestone would have been scraped away by glaciers in most areas of the state, but here it was, a small window into the history of this landscape unmarked by the direct influence of the Ice Age.

DJ found a reed the color of straw and held it between his teeth. The reed extended about five feet, so he had to jut his lower jaw to keep the stalk from dragging on the trail. Walking casually with his thumbs hooked in his belt loops and his jacket unzipped, he waited for me to notice. My attention was divided. He was ready to engage me, but even with his on-again/off-again interest in talking to me, I looked out to the river's currents, frozen in patterns of blue and white. The dam and open waters were just at the edges of our vision to the south and to the north where the eagles should have been.

When I turned to DJ to throw up my hands in frustration, he raised one eyebrow, pushed up the brim of his baseball cap with his index finger and spoke through clenched teeth. "Howdy, ma'am. That's a right perty ski jacket you're a wearin'."

"I wore it for you. I know how you love to see me in goose down."

He reached with his thumb and index finger, mimicking some old black and white movie cowboy, pulled the stalk from between his teeth, and threw it to the ground. "That's right nice of ya."

His silliness stopped, and our path along the cliff ended. I stood in desperation, willing my eyes to see something. My binoculars kept the scope of my vision small, and I didn't see the big buzzard coming. DJ nudged my arm. I lowered the glasses and saw dark wings and then the red face: a turkey vulture, flying upriver. The buzzard's head is nearly devoid of feathers, which comes in handy when it's inside some rotting carcass. This vulture's face looked raw and bloody, as if it had been skinned, so he looked normal for a turkey vulture. Ornithologists have reclassified this scavenger as a stork relative, but I've never seen this vulture's ugly face on any baby shower invitation. This is not an avifauna I wanted to get close to. To wit: when they feel threatened, they regurgitate, perhaps an adaptation to lighten their stomach load for a quick getaway. In any event, this vulture shouldn't have been here. It was nearly January; it should have migrated south weeks ago. Either something was wrong with the bird—it was old, blind, or sick—or this was a sign of global warming, or maybe this bird was a maverick. As we watched the deep V of his wings in a wobbling flight pattern and the dramatic darkness of his bulk, I had to admit that he was impressive. Calls of smaller birds from the trees behind us turned me around.

DJ zipped his coat and followed me to the stands of black walnuts, oaks, elms, and maples. Golden and purple finches flew into the prairie as we left it. My winter favorites busied themselves in the tracks of forest. Chickadees moved in swarms and called to one other. At least two kinds of woodpeckers drummed at the hardwoods, one tapping and one hammering. When we stood very quietly, the variation in percussion was audible. Three kinds—red-bellied, downy, and hairy woodpeckers— showed themselves. Cardinals whistled and flashed their scarlet feathers. Nuthatches roamed the tree trunks, and juncos twinkled their hidden black and white tail stripes when we flushed them from the ground. It would be possible to walk through these hardwoods and miss the life here, but once accustomed to looking, you see life everywhere.

When the trail brought us back to the bluff, we found ourselves looking to overcast and empty skies. We walked the edge of the bluff, which curved in toward at the point where we stood. I leaned in defeat against the wide trunk of an old oak. Where were they? Eagles faithfully nest in the areas of their birth, but they are opportunistic migrators and go where food is easiest to obtain in winter. Why did so few come back this year? We heard rumors in town that the gizzard shad population was down. The adult shad is a favorite of the eagle. Who knew if the shad were in a normal cycle of ebb and flow or if their diminished numbers signaled a devastating trend? According to local papers, ornithologists were not worried about the decline at this point. If fewer eagles came back to the river; they could have just dispersed over a wider area this winter. But we knew the scientists would be watching the nesting populations closely this spring. No one with an understanding of the past takes bald eagles for granted anymore.

The Mississippi has changed course about every 1,000 years. The normal flooding and runoff of land endows the riverbed with the seeds of its own destruction. Silt and dirt carried by high-water runoff fills the riverbed, but in previous ages, before civilization and its many dominions, the impetus of the water just carved out a new path. Slight variations and dramatic shifts in the course of the river were no longer a part of the valley's self-management. Scientists are still studying the cycles of the flora and fauna of the region and trying to discover how to mimic the natural sequence. The truth is, we still don't really understand how to manage this resource, but we won't let the ecosystem take charge: developed land would be lost.

I stretched up to touch the underside of a thick branch that reached out toward the river. DJ helped me pull a picnic table over, telling me, "You go first." Soon we both sat upon the sturdy oak, watching and waiting. Within a few minutes, an eagle passed directly in our line of sight, immature with mottled white and brown tail and head feathers. The alabaster speckles told me that this one was nearly grown, about four years old. We straddled the tree branch, DJ in front, and we waited. He didn't turn around to face me, but spoke over the bluff. "I'm worried about football. What if you ruined things for me?"

I didn't understand at first and hadn't then realized that the same Mr. Ehrlich who opposed the Grimsley play was an assistant football coach who'd taken a special interest in my son. "Go on."

"He could keep me from playing first string. I know that's not as important as your free speech thing."

I said, "Mr. Ehrlich isn't going to punish you because I don't agree with him," but I thought, *Oh shit.* DJ shouldn't have to pay the price for my big mouth. My second thought was that Mr. Ehrlich believed he was doing the right thing as strongly as I believed he was totally wrong. He did care about the kids and wanted to protect them. I understood his desire to keep children innocent as long as possible, but my sense of reality told me that the delusion that we have created a safe world for our children lasts only while we hold them in our arms. We don't want to pull back the curtain and reveal the ills of the world, because then we are no longer authors of only great acts. Before our children become the central actors, I believe we have to discuss and confront horrid realities.

My disagreement with Ehrlich didn't make him an enemy. DJ, at last, looked at me. "He really helped me in football practice. Is it okay for me to like him?"

Before I could answer, three mature bald eagles soared along the opposite side of the cliff, but we kept talking as our eyes tracked the flight. I told DJ he could like him.

Cold humidity seeped in and seemed to turn the synovial fluid in my joints into an icy slush. I started to fidget and rubbed my hands for warmth. The nearby outhouse began to inspire fond thoughts. When I climbed down from the tree, DJ stayed perched above me. As my feet reached the picnic table, one immense eagle soared slowly, directly in front of our faces, as if she wanted to get a good look at us. She followed the curve in the bluff, rising on the air current displaced by the mass of the river valley wall. We saw it all: the nostril notch and hook in the end of her strong yellow bill, her stark white head feathers lying so the nap of her light plumage overlapped her dark carinate body, her slightly down-turned tail feathers, her beefy legs and obsidian talons, her fierce open eye, and a seven-foot wing span with the tips turned slightly back. The bird seemed to claim dominion over the valley, yet her species was still threatened. We watched until she flew down to the dam and through the cloudy warmth rising from the open water.

THE POINT OF FEBRUARY

"If I had influence with the good fairy who is supposed to preside over the christening of all children, I should ask that her gift to each child in the world be a sense of wonder so indestructible that it would last throughout life."
RACHEL CARSON

In the flow of a forgotten sentence, while appreciating a soaring red-tailed hawk and the silver shadows of a snow-covered meadow, my skis fired forward, and I fell into a childbirth position, supine and bent-kneed. The fall became a physical manifestation of a recurrent dream. Instead of examining the apparitional scene that tried to push its way into conscious consideration (the ugly flowered gown and the white sheet covering my knees, the empty feeling, and the crowd of onlookers), I decided to fix my eyes on the full moon rising over a field of strong brown and red sedges. It shone over a remnant of summer grasses and reeds that stood firm though half-buried in snow. As if accustomed to viewing the moon from a fall-induced position, I pointed to the sky and said, "Look, the last full moon of winter."

My eleven-year-old son skied with me, lured by a promise that he would see a few of Wisconsin's Native American pointing trees. DJ briefly looked up at the moon, confidently shifted his weight from one ski to the other, and huffed. "I was worried you hurt yourself, and you lay there and enjoy the view."

I knew getting up couldn't be a nonchalant rising that would reestablish my dignity. While of trio of slim athletes strode by in alpine race suits,

I pretended not to care that I had to remove my skis to rise. DJ laughed when I rocked like an overturned turtle trying to get off my back while heavily laden with winter clothes. I laughed too, loudly so the skimeisters would know I wasn't hurt and wouldn't come over and offer to help. I had never noticed the precise moment when I lost my athletic poise, but it was gone. Somewhere in the years of mothering two children, long work hours, volunteer work, perpetual college courses, a wicked ankle fracture in my thirties, and years of generally letting myself go, I lost the ability to swan dive, run a six-thirty mile, and lift my keister out of the wet snow with strong, limber muscles.

No damage done from the fall. We were off to cross-country ski and find the Native American Marker trees of Lapham Peak. I wanted DJ to see two particular pointing trees, and I wanted to share the splinter of information that I recalled from my grade school days and adult questionings. Native Americans tied hardwood saplings to the ground. As the sapling grew, it resumed its tendency toward vertical growth, leaving a horizontal (or nearly horizontal) section of trunk. That horizontal segment formed one side of guiding point and inspired the name of the trees. As I remembered it, a 1950s photo in an old school book was captioned, "Indian pointing trees on a hunting path near Lapham Peak." Doodles of these two trees decorated the margins of my schoolgirl notebook. I began each sketch by drawing pairs of exaggerated chevrons standing on end to illustrate the trunks, and then added the scaffolding of branches, and leaves if the season called for them. Memories of the image reappeared in the landscapes of my adult dreams. The trees carried a resonance of myth. I saw the pointers in person only when I was past thirty, but have visited them every two or three years since then. When I was a child, I sometimes imagined a strong brave in MGM-style buckskin tying the tree with bark lashings to point to the place of buffalo congregation. As the trail lights came on and augmented the shadows of the forest, I imagined a leathery elder, bundled in bear hide, tying a spring sapling to the ground with hopes that the tree would some day direct her descendents to the lake country rich in perch, duck, and deer.

Ever since they were saplings, these trees stood in witness to people walking near this trail and using the high vantage point of the peak. In 1851, Charles Hanson built an observation tower at the highest point in the area. He charged visitors to climb and enjoy the view and to picnic in the lush forest. About twenty years later, Increase A. Lapham, who had been petitioning the government to establish a weather service, used the tower as a signal station to receive meteorological signals from Pike's Peak in Colorado and relay reports on the incoming weather to the Great Lakes ports. In addition to being known as the father of the US Weather Bureau, Lapham surveyed the land, trees, shellfish, and Indian mounds, publishing his findings in scientific journals across the nation. He wrote damning warnings about the clear-cut logging practices that were ignored until the great white pines of the north and the hardwoods of the south, as well as the state's logging-based economy, were all close to being wiped out. Predictably, Lapham's forebodings were appreciated only after the devastation of the forest.

A tower still stood at this highest point in Waukesha County. I didn't care to climb the tower to see the view adulterated by mansions, strip malls, and the new one-million-square-foot department store distribution center. Months ago, when I first saw the dark roofs and parking lots of the industrial areas, I wondered why the warehouse couldn't be built on the already depredated and abandoned land in the city. There, the building and jobs could do more good than harm. Our local system of government has no process to consider wise regional use of land. When I climb the high tower and see the broken forests and profligate development, I feel a kinship with a Native Chief that I have no right to feel: my ancestors stole this land. Lakota Chief Black Elk said:

> "I did not know then how much was ended. When I look back now from this high hill of my old age, I can still see the butchered women and children lying heapen and scattered all along the crooked gulch as plain as when I saw them with eyes still young. And I can see that something else died there in the bloody mud, and was buried in the blizzard. A people's dream died there. It was a beautiful dream…the nation's hoop is broken and scattered. There is no center any longer, and the sacred tree is dead."

Although DJ did not ask, I told him I did not want to climb the observation tower to see the bright lights of the lake country.

The trail was groomed widely enough for DJ to competently imitate the skate-style skiing we saw as racers tore past us in wide distance-eating pushes over the undulating terrain. Conversely, I followed the tracks of a white-haired skier who'd passed during my tumble. My shuffle did transition to a glide. DJ skied beyond the boundaries of my vision. I'd catch an occasional glimpse of him, peering over his shoulder to make eye contact with me before he tore off again in an open-throttle disappearing act. We skied under the rising moon the Potawatomi called a "full hunger" moon: February being the month of heavy snows, depleted resources, and the final month before spring. The evening did not conjure thoughts of spring. It seemed instead, with the calm winds, thirty-degree temperatures, and milky incandescent forest, like winter had just ripened to perfection.

Our trail in the Kettle Moraine State Forest snaked across the terminal moraines of the Green Bay and Michigan lobes of the Wisconsin Glacier and also crossed the ancient drainage ways, leaving behind a severely textured land. Over 10,000 years ago, when the ice sheets began their final retreat, this land was shaped by the gravel, silt, and boulders shoved and left behind. It was shaped as well by the immense runoff of released water after thousands of years ensnared in an icy-blue terrestrial berg. DJ waited for me as the skiing got more challenging.

An irregularly hilly terrain hid dozens of secret garden meadows among the cover of the dense forest plots. I told DJ that if someone asked me what I really wanted, like Mary in *The Secret Garden*, I'd ask for "a bit of earth." And I'd like it on the shore of a small, unspoiled lake. My mom bought a house on one of the many lakes near here after I was grown. I still dream of my morning swims across the lake with my collie. I remembered the ice-skating party there, how my date knelt in front of me to tie my skates, and how I began to fall in love with the man I'd marry on that frozen water.

When Mom moved to Florida, we couldn't afford to buy the home from her. I often fought the urge to lament that I didn't live in a southern Wisconsin lake cottage on a wooded lot with people I love, at least one smart dog, and a small garden. But there weren't many small homes blending into these mixed hardwood forests. As the original cottages were sold, many were demolished and replaced with massive homes, garages, and patios. In the process of bringing luxury to these woods, the wealthy chased out the wildness with the concrete and chemical footprints of hubris.

In my dreams, I see a small cottage placed in a woodland understory with a sunny opening at the entrance to the water. A small overturned canoe rests on a grassy bank, and in the distance, the two pointing trees aim at our lake home.

Our ski trail existed because the State Forests protected some of land and habitats from the metastasis of mansions, patios, and Jet Skis. As my weight shifted from one foot to the other, I felt the sinuosity of the earth and a sense of intimacy that deepened as the sun dipped below the horizon and the shadows softened. DJ tired of my slow pace and moved to the center of the trail. As soon as he again began the muscular push-off strides, his body sputtered, and although he fought for control, he landed on his back.

"You okay?" I asked.

At first, he didn't answer, but stared upward. "You're right. There is a full moon, and there's a planet. Jupiter, I think." As he got up, quickly and without removing his skis, he talked about his Spanish teacher. "She told us today we all acted loco, like there was going to be a full moon tonight. What's the deal with a full moon?"

I explained that when the moon is full or new, the sun and moon line up and their gravitational pull works together. These are the times that the moon and earth are most attracted to each other. The earth holds on to all its mass, but water strains and bows its malleable shape toward the moon, causing high tides. Water does not care if it is in an ocean, Lake Michigan, or a living cell; it all responds to the tug. Science cannot prove we go crazy or fall in love or act more stupid than normal during these full moons or tides that are called "spring tides" no matter the season.

Science can only prove the tug of our full moon is real.

DJ swiped some snow off his butt. "That tug is pretty strong tonight, huh?"

We reached the top of a hill and turned onto a rolling path of natural moguls. White spruce bowed their dense lower branches in submission to the previous night's heavy snowfall. Many of the branches were broken. This winter pruning would allow the sun to reach spring blossoms on the forest floor. I skied in tracks at the edge of the path, where pines would brush my clothes and release the fresh resin scent of winter.

DJ stood waiting for me, not complaining, nor did he respond when I said, "Sorry I'm so slow."

When we were moving together again, he said, "Those were white pines. I counted the needles." I was pleased he remembered the Scout lesson that five letters in the word *white* matched the five-needled cup, though he quickly changed the subject. "Where are the Indian trees?"

"I'm not sure, but keep looking. We must be getting close. I think they are a few hundred yards past that trail." An "Ice Age Trail" sign marked a path that crossed our ski course. The Ice Age Trail treks 1,000 miles through the state, the realized dream of thousands of volunteers who work to preserve the unique landscape at the terminal edge of glacial advance. Back in the 1950s, lawyer Raymond Zillmer began to lobby and organize resources and support for his project. He established a foundation to acquire and maintain a footpath along the ancient glacial edge in a protected and unmolested habitat. The foundation still works to convince land owners to preserve and deed access to the trail and to raise money to buy land with Zillmer's words, "We spend millions to go fast; let's spend a little to go slow." The Ice Age Trail is now recognized, along with the Continental Divide Trail, The Appalachian Trail, Natchez Trace Trail, Potomac Heritage Trail, and others as a National Scenic Trail. The protected footpaths and parks and forests give me a place to feel free from the salesmanship of civilization. Here, I'm removed from pressures to possess, upgrade, and hoard. Zillmer's trail, Muir's Sierra Nevada, the Nature Conservancy's protected land, and National and State Parks, Forests, and Trusts are essential islands of reality. We need more.

The trail ahead began a dramatic downward slope and curve. I watched DJ sashay, accelerate, fall, and quickly get up again without looking back. He rode the hill to the base. Then he turned to watch me. I didn't think I had much of a chance of making it down, even though I planned to widen the distance between my skis and tuck down to make myself more stable. Worried about running into a tree, I aimed so that if I couldn't take the curve, I'd only hit a bush, not one of the wide oaks or red pines that crowded the trail. The momentum and slickness of the hill overtook my ability to turn, so I dragged my poles to slow down but couldn't get my ski tips pointed inward to snowplow myself into a stop. I ended up lying on my back with my legs straddling a bush. The branches of the shrub held little orbs of ice that glowed in the overhead moonlight like the crystal drops of a chandelier.

DJ yelled up from the bottom of the hill. "Sure is a beautiful full moon, huh?"

"It looks especially nice from under this bush. Did you know there's a sheet of ice under this snow?"

"You just noticed that?"

I'd been sticking to the edges of the trail and hadn't seen what should have been obvious. We'd originally planned this trip for yesterday morning, before a storm arrived as sleet and then stuck around as a road-closing winter storm. Although we'd set the alarm for seven, by seven-thirty, we'd postponed the trip. When I surrendered to a lingering cold and lay down on top of my made bed, DJ grabbed a chenille throw from the chair and joined me. He turned on the TV while I curled into a fetal position and began to doze. He woke me up with a little squeeze that I interpreted as a snuggle. He corrected me, telling me he was trying to get me to stop snoring.

DJ had found the movie *Psycho*. By the time I realized what he was watching, it was only minutes before the shower scene. I decided to encourage him to watch for fine direction—how we didn't really see the violence, but the small details dramatized within the violent act. As a child, this shower scene had scared me into a two-day accumulation of body odor, but DJ didn't look the least bit traumatized. During the commercial he told me that even though it was an old movie in black and white, he thought movie close-ups were great and how the popping of each shower curtain ring let the audience know that nothing could help this girl; she was going down.

DJ yelled up the hill to the halfway-down point where I lay. "You going to get up or what?" Before I moved out of childbirth position, the dream pushed into my awareness, the crowd around me chanting, "Push, push, push!" I opened my eyes and focused my mind on our surroundings.

By the time I caught up to DJ, he'd lost his momentum and plodded along with me, watching the woods for unusual trees. We had passed by deer and rabbit tracks, but stopped to examine four animal prints that looked like a handprint of a skinny thumb and the two closest fingers— an owl. Bending down close to the shoulder of the trail, we saw the faint clusters of polka dots from little toes with a line running between them that mixed in with the owl prints. The tracks ended suddenly, the drama emphasized by a slate of undisturbed snow. A mouse, dragging its tail in the snow, had been snatched.

Still huddling over the tracks, DJ said, "Just like *Psycho*."

"Do you mean murder?"

"No. I mean great use of detail."

When we stood up, the background moved into the foreground, and two Native American pointing trees stood directly in front of us. These trees bent westward and then vertically in precise synchrony. Two oaks stood ready to direct the wanderer to rich hunting grounds. The trees had grown tall by the nineteenth century, when Potawatomi were struggling to survive in a state where the Indian policy was to scatter, relocate, and exterminate natives and their claims to the land. Many Native Americans ended up working for the logging companies, and some were able to buy land in northern counties. Potawatomi ("keepers of the fire") is the name whites gave the tribe. The tribe calls themselves *Neshnabek*, which means "the true people" or "ones who know." Behind the trees stood mature red pines, grown to be harvested for telephone poles. The two ancients remained. In my memory of the black and white picture, they stood in front of a field of grasses and the stumps of clear-cut land. The two had been spared out of respect (or perhaps the unusual shape made them difficult to harvest).

DJ wanted to know more about the trees, but there just wasn't much to tell. I'd tried to research the pointers and found an Illinois artist, Dennis Downes, whose career centered on natural antiquities. He had hiked out here with me and brought back botanical experts to check out the trees. He told me these trail trees were 200–300 years old and had lived so long by growing slowly in the glacial gravel. Dennis didn't know why there would be two so close together. He'd never seen this before, yet they looked authentic to him. The Milwaukee Museum historian didn't have much to offer me. "Yes, there are marker trees out there." I explained to DJ that I couldn't find a native source to specifically explain the trees to me. That exploration didn't lead to much factual information. One email from someone who called himself "Red Hawk" from Spirit Talk came back to me from multiple inquiries. Red Hawk said, "Oki Amy, I am going to give you a starting point, and from there you should be able to find your way to information about your trees of the lake country." He led me to information about the tribal belief that behind all individual spirits and personifications of the divine, there is a single creative life force, sometimes called the "Great Mystery." This force manifests itself throughout the universe in every human, animal, rock, atom, grain of sand, and tree. Every story, too, is a working out of this life force. Red Hawk never mentioned the pointing trees. I thought "Oki," the way he started my email, was a typo, that he'd meant to say, "Okay." I discovered later that oki is a native word for "water," which still didn't completely negate the possibility of an errant I. DJ thought this Red Hawk guy must have known me and made no mistake, because I loved to be near, in, and on water. Red Hawk didn't return any more emails. Apparently, he felt he'd fully answered my questions about the pointing trees of this lake country. And of course he had, because the meaning of natural antiquities is not found solely in words, but also in experiences.

DJ and I stood and stared. He put his hands on his hips. "So the Indians tied saplings to the ground hundreds of years ago, and the trees grew to have trunks that point. We think they are pointing to good land. "

"Yep."

"And the trees are still here?"

"Yep. The trees are still pointing."

After I turned forty, I began to have a recurrent dream. The first time the dream visited, I knew it wasn't ordinary because it didn't leave as morning, day, and life busied my mind. This is the dream that never left:

> A crowd surrounds me. In the foreground, I see my husband Paul, daughter Andrea, son DJ, parents, PattiJo, and other good friends. Aunts, uncles, cousins, and workmates are all discernable, but they blend into a mass of unrecognizable faces. Everyone stares between my legs. A hospital gown "decorated" with poorly forged blue flowers snaps at my neck. A sheet is tented around my flexed knees. Before a masked obstetrician pushes the drape aside, DJ and some of the men in the group move to the head of the bed to preserve my modesty.
>
> My husband smiles and in his soft-spoken way urges me on, "Push, honey."
>
> I hear the voices in the crowd. My daughter Andrea wants another brother, but my DJ thinks a little sister would be great. To others, it doesn't matter, "as long as it's healthy."
>
> Voices of the critical waft in beyond the up close smiling faces. "She doesn't seem to be pushing very hard. Isn't it time something happened?"
>
> I act like I'm pushing, but I know something they don't: there is no baby. I stop straining and open my eyes to see two sticks in the white horizon. They become the center of my focus. I recognize the two pointing trees.

My youngest offspring is leaving childhood. I've crossed over to middle age. My worth as a human is not based in reproduction; I will do no more to propel my genes into the future through childbirth. Biologically, if not spiritually, my *raison d'être* is to care for and protect the earth, so that my life will flow and reside in future generations. I am a water woman who grew babies in the amniotic sea beneath my breath. I live in a chronologically advancing awareness of my final reconciliation with the earth. The big house we worked so hard for is now too big. We've let the lawn fill with clover. The mall and television fail to draw my attention. What calls? The chickadee and the hawk, the ice and snow, the changing hues of the sky, the naked trees and the pines, the lakes, and the shifting celestial bodies. I reside in phases and tides.

My genes are successful nucleotides, *Homo sapiens* were fruitful. We multiplied. We filled the earth. The biologic drive to reproduce and raise children is essential to survival of the species, but it is a worthless effort without a healthy planet. Not that I frequently consider my genes, but I do think of my children, Andrea and DJ. And I think of their children and the communities and cultures that share the planet. My purpose is to nourish the earth, to point my descendants to a way and a land where they may thrive. Thriving is no longer a numbers game; we have enough people. Much of the planet is plundered. I must learn to save and restore what I can—to discover the constituents of a life lived in support of the earth. Like the Native American who used her rope to tether a sapling that would take decades to grow large enough to mark the trail, I must think beyond my days. This drive might be genetic, but it feels spiritual.

My dream does not end neatly. I always wake up. If I were to script the dream, my children and the crowd would look away from me and to the two pointing trees. I'd get up off the table, and we would all follow the simple directions to good land.

DJ took off to ride the last part of the trail named "The Magic Carpet Ride" and yelled back to me, "Come on, Mom. I'm getting hungry, and you promised to buy me dinner." He began the run of smooth dips and rises and passed into one of the depressions and beyond my sight. I didn't try to catch up.

SECOND DATE WITH THE APOSTLES

*"When we see land as a community to which we belong,
we may begin to use it with love and respect."*

ALDO LEOPOLD

Steve Dunker, the local bookstore owner, told us to go: "You have to walk to the ice caves." He pushed aside the aged hardcover he'd been reading and reached for a county road map. "Since you already went to Madeline, your next step would be to take Highway 13 out of Bayfield. Before you get to Corn, you'll see a sign for Meyers Lake Road. There should be some people tracks for you to follow through the woods for a couple of miles. You'll come out near the shoreline."

The hotline at the Apostle Islands National Lakeshore had already told us that the Lake Superior ice at the floor of the caves was unsafe. According to Steve, "They always say that." He looked up from the county road map spread across the walnut counter and searched my eyes for an acknowledgement that I understood his directions.

Bayfield Books/What Goes 'Round occupied half of a white and yellow clapboard building. An arts and crafts gallery shared a wall with this store. When we opened the door to tall stacks of books and labeled shelves, the slope of the dark hardwood floor pitched us inward. Every space was covered in books, both worn and new. The store didn't smell of dust or mildew like so many resale shops do, but of wood. The building, floors, shelves, and inventory all retained the scent of their origin.

I tapped the map's Lake Superior Shoreline. "The ice is safe? You're sure?"

Steve looked to me and then nodded to my eleven-year-old son as he spoke: "Anytime you step on the ice, it's a risk."

DJ and I had come to the Wisconsin shores of Lake Superior for a weekend trip, and at only ten-thirty in the morning, we felt we'd already had too big a share of ice and danger. We'd never visited this area of the state in the winter. Stories of ice caves and the frozen road on the surface of the largest body of fresh water in the world drew us from the southeast corner of the state. Seven hours on the road meant our weekend was only one day long when we took into account the Friday night drive and Sunday morning departure. So, on the first Saturday in March, we rose early to have our winter day near and on the immense lake famous for beauty and infamous for its fury.

Ashland's proximity to the shore surprised us in the morning when we stepped out of the hotel to drive to Bayfield. Directly across a two-lane highway, the ice of Lake Superior's Chequamegon Bay completely filled our field of vision. In the darkness of the previous night, we hadn't realized we'd been driving Superior's shores for hours; we'd only seen as far as our headlights illuminated. Several summers ago, we arrived by a different road. I tried to remind DJ about Bayfield and the Apostle Island National Lakeshore, which is made up of both islands and shoreline, and described the town, the Victorian homes, and the jungled flower boxes. DJ could only remember the car ferry we took to Madeline Island and the rented cabin where we ate spaghetti two nights in a row because Dad made so much. DJ loves spaghetti.

A memory of standing in the Bayfield sun while waiting for the ferry came over me. The August breeze and its undercurrent of a chill on an otherwise sunny eighty-five degree day had evoked trepidation. Alaska's summer breeze had passed a similar chill across my skin. That preternatural Lake Superior wind gave me the creeps.

I'd always preferred a small lake—a lake where I could see the shore, the waves couldn't lap over my head, and an overturned canoe could be fun instead of lethal. Lake Superior has an average temperature of about forty degrees Fahrenheit and doesn't deviate more than about six degrees all year. Being a good swimmer in Lake Superior wouldn't help me anymore than in the seawaters of the Gulf of Alaska, which I'd carefully kayaked. I lived in Alaska about the same time John McPhee moved into the largest state and celebrated its proportions in *Coming into the Country*, but I'd left after three years. Although I wouldn't have admitted it at the time, Alaska made me feel small and vulnerable. As much as I loved its severe beauty, and as much as I sought wild experiences and tried to see as much as I could, anxieties of a wrong step on a glacier, a chance encounter with a grizzly, a plunge into the frigid Pacific, or a betrayal by an impotent alternator on a wilderness road shadowed me on almost every outdoor experience. The only place I ever felt at ease was the one-mile walk along the ALCAN Highway to the Diehl's Grocery store where I worked. I knew those drunken pines, summer wild roses, and that there was just enough traffic to discourage the bears. In late May, when the moose dropped their calves and the bears were more excitable, I'd get a ride to work. I couldn't be carefree in most of Alaska. The chill from Lake Superior reminded me of a breeze coming off Beluga Bay near the Turnagain arm of Cook Inlet. My Alaska uneasiness superimposed itself onto the shores and water of the Ojibwe tribe's Gitche Gumee.

I'd read that February and the beginning of March were the times we'd most likely be able to drive on the lake to Madeline Island and to walk near the mainland to see the ice caves. The late winter air didn't hold much bite, and the comfort in the air worried us. Our van's thermometer read the outside temperature as thirty-two degrees. We drove to Bayfield to check out the ice road that replaces the ferry service every winter when the ice is safe. Ice shanties speckled the lake surface, but DJ kept reading the van's thermometer, thirty-three, thirty-four, and then thirty-five degrees by the time I parked in the ferry service parking lot near a hand-painted sign with the crooked words "Ice Unsafe."

Bayfield's coolness had frightened me in the summer, and the climbing temperatures of late winter lessened my bravado to drive directly onto the ice, so we investigated by walking onto the frozen lake road. Cars, trucks, and ice shanties sat halfway to Madeline Island, and several cars drove by us as we stood at the edge of the road. Cut evergreens, having completed their work as Christmas trees, were planted in snow banks, which lined and marked the official road. We stood at the edge of the road and watched vehicles pass us as they drove over the icy lake from the island to the mainland. I waved down a passing car and asked about the ice road. The driver assured me he lived on the island and the ice was "plenty thick."

As we walked back to the cars, I did see a more official-looking sign propped and tied onto a stack of tires that read, "Cars and light trucks only." This sign was printed in the color and font of other authoritative street signs that I regularly obeyed. DJ and I agreed it seemed safe to drive the two miles to the largest of the Apostle Islands. DJ watched the ice-bound docks in the marina recede as we advanced on the lake, commenting, "This is weird."

I wished I couldn't see the sealed cracks in the ice, but I didn't hear creaking or feel any give in the road. Still, I reached my hand to the mesh basket between the front seats, feeling for the hammer I'd insisted my husband buy in case the electric windows and doors shorted out if the van ever plunged underwater. DJ watched our crystalline lane and the ice fishing activity beyond the shoulder of the road. He asked me how thick I thought the ice was. I answered, "Oh, at least a few feet," but did not mention that Lake Superior's average depth is almost 500 feet. I didn't know at the time that the ice was only a few inches thick. This Great Lake is known as a lake that does not give up her dead. It never warms up enough to allow a body's intestinal bacteria to proliferate, produce gas, and float the body to the surface.

I also didn't tell DJ that I'd read that the ice break-up usually occurs at twenty-five feet from shore, especially as we passed the spot about twenty-five feet from the shore of Madeline Island. The ice highway had been known to break up in a matter of hours. When I told DJ about the Ojibwe lore of a great horned lynx that lived under the ice (Mishipeshu), we both looked to the frosty road covering a dark world we didn't know. It was easier to picture the horns of a giant sea-god rising up and splitting open the thick white cladding than to fathom a wind so blusterous it could tear up the frozen crust of this freshwater sea. Gusts do cross these open waters and capitalize on up to 200 momentum-building miles to generate destructive wind and waves.

The ice road transitioned to asphalt as we crept up the strong back of Madeline Island, and we arrived at the only Apostle Island with roads and cars. Madeline, the largest of the islands at twenty-four square miles, is not a designated part of the Apostle Islands National Lakeshore. The island is under development, and here, individuals can own land and live in the northernmost year-round homes in Wisconsin. None of the other twenty-one islands in the Apostle archipelago have paved roads or privately owned land or homes. When humans overnight on the other islands, they walk and camp. Previous human habitation and exploitation had scarred almost every one of the Apostles. All the early settlers and heartache homesteaders, who couldn't domesticate this land, left years before the creation of the National Lakeshore Park. Old-growth forests remain in only the most inaccessible locations and around some of the lighthouses, where logging was prohibited to assure lighthouse keepers access to firewood. Most of the islands' land and shores have been rewilding for over 100 years, and mature second-growth forests tower above the lakeshore obscuring the old images of clear-cut land. On five of the islands, the forests were never cut. Out of our reach, unmolested wilderness did exist.

More snowmobiles than cars seemed to purr around the town of La Pointe, where we saw activity at only one gas pump (not a whole station—just one lone pump outside a small store) and two restaurants. The Historical Museum was closed. We'd learned on our summer visit that it was constructed from a surviving building of the American Fur Company, part of a resident's barn and the old La Pointe jail. I reminded DJ that our family legend on my dad's side claims we are related to Ramsey Crooks, who was in charge of and later owned the American Fur Company. He did business in that very building in the early 1800s.

DJ looked skeptical. "Did Grandpa Dan tell you that?"

"Well, that's the story, and Grandpa Dan is a Crooks."

The island's known history reached back to the Ojibwe and French fur traders who were setting up trade on this island when the Mayflower was landing near Plymouth Rock. The fur traders tended to take Ojibwe wives and adopt their customs, which had helped both the Ojibwe and the traders to prosper in the Lake Superior area. Fur trade prospered as long as Native Americans controlled the land. Ojibwe called the island *Moningwunakauning*, "The Home of the Golden Breasted Woodpecker," either a northern flicker or a yellow-bellied sapsucker.

We passed the golf course, and I gave it a sneer. Building a golf course on a small island prized for its wild beauty seemed profane. I couldn't understand why someone would leave their more urban existence, enticed by this Superior archipelago, and find enjoyment playing golf on this land cleared of its wilderness. It was easy for me to be critical; I wasn't trying to make a living from land ownership here. I didn't believe, however, that Theodore S. Gary, a descendent of early island landowners who had the course built in the 1960s, was hurting for money when he planned the course on the ancient site of an Ojibwe village.

After driving a few blocks, we left the town and every car and snowmobile. The roads were plowed, and although 250 residents spend at least part of their winter on this island, we didn't see another car or person. The small homes and cottages fit into the understory of the tall surrounding pines and mature hardwoods.

When South Shore Drive approached a clearing near Chebornnicon Bay, the shoreline startled me into an abrupt stop. DJ didn't have to ask why. He just said, "Whoa!" Hundreds of slabs of baby blue chunks of ice were piled high along the entire beach, like gigantic rocks of blue topaz and aquamarine, lit from within. Their color matched the hue of glacial ice. When light travels into thin ice, it is reflected back without any particular color preference within the light spectrum, and all the light is reflected off the surface as white. I explained to DJ that when light travels a longer path into coarser and thicker ice, more red and yellow light is absorbed, leaving blue light to illuminate the iridescent blocks.

Looking out from the side of the island that took the brunt of Lake

Superior's weather, it was easy to see how the blue slabs were formed. Winter temperatures froze the surface in one- to two-foot-thick sheets, and then those gales roughed it up and pushed the chunks onto the beach. The forested island served as a windbreak, allowing the smooth ice to accumulate on the other side of the island where people trusted the trees to protect them as they drove the ice road between Bayfield and Madeline.

We drove the fourteen-mile length and three-mile width of island, stopping and exploring whenever we felt like it. On one of our stops, we made the only footprints into a woodland of second-growth jack pines. Each pine stood with perfect posture, columns in a forest cathedral. The needled branches began about twelve feet from the ground, leaving sturdy archetypal trunks in the dark shade of the pine boughs. The ground, likely covered in ferns in summer, held a clean slate of fresh snow, as did the branches above. When the wind shuffled the branches, twinkles of light and snow sifted down as if we were encased in a freshly shaken snow globe. On the way back to the car, DJ stepped out of the shadows into the warmth of the sun and splashed into a puddle of slush. He looked up at me and said, "I think we better get back before the road melts."

At the end of the island and the beginning of the ice road, a handmade sign placed askew did not block the road, but stood ready about twenty feet away from its entrance and warned, "Ice Road Closed." The Superior ice still looked as busy as when we'd come. The road was just barely open.

If the road closed, the only way off the island would be by wind-sled, which does not transport cars, only people. DJ read the thermometer. "Thirty-seven!" He pointed to puddles of slush on the shoulder of the road, but we drove across the lake to Bayfield.

The thought suddenly occurred to me that the sign at the Bayfield side of the ice road had said "Cars and light trucks only." We drove a van. I wondered out loud, "Is a van lighter than a light truck? It must be. Don't you think?" I distracted DJ (and myself) by pointing to the red sandstone cliffs that rimmed the frosted lake. We'd boated close to similar crimson cliffs on Devil's and Sand Islands when we visited the different islands and lighthouses in summer but never got close to any of the arched and vaulted caves and pillars. Where islands didn't serve as barriers to diminish winds and waves, the ruddled cliffs were exposed to the full measure of the lake's ferocious wind and weather. The same pummeling waves that had worn away the iron-oxide-rich sandstone, drawing tourists to the lithic landmarks, also washed angrily into caverns. The waves here could break up a kayak in summer and sweep away the ice floor in winter. Sometimes the waves crashed with such velocity they entered caves, tunnels, and crevices and thundered through openings above like unscheduled geysers.

Once we arrived back on the mainland, DJ and I didn't have a plan. The ice caves seemed out of the question. He wondered if there was a movie theater in Bayfield, but I insisted that we go for a hike in one of the nearby forests. We needed to walk if we were to begin to know this land. The county map was a collage of color: green for the Chequamegon-Nicolet National Forest, yellow for state land, peach for Bayfield County Forest, blue for Apostle Islands National Lake Shore, violet for non-motorized wilderness area, pink for USDA Forest Service, and slash marks for the Red Cliff Reservation Boundaries. All the trails we'd found on Madeline had been groomed for cross-country skiing, so we needed to know where, in all these miles of forest, we'd find a trail okay for foot travel. The Bayfield Visitor Center was open, but neither the brochures that promised "a year-round-playground of fun" nor the unattended information counter could point us to a trail. Most of the businesses were closed; some were so closed that the "closed for the season" signs were decipherable only by the tops of the letters that broke cover from the crest of the snow banks.

Bayfield Books/What Goes 'Round, with its concrete shoveled walk, looked more open than anything else in town. The smallness and fullness of the store made poking around seem mandatory. DJ settled into browsing as quickly as I did. I planned to ask about foot trails when we checked out.

When Steve asked if he could help, I inquired about local natural history books. He walked to the shelves, touching the spines and listing the names of those he especially liked. We browsed for a good half hour, and I found a mushroom identification book I'd been wanting. I had thought I was getting one for Christmas, but apparently neither my husband nor son could believe I'd really be happy with the gift of fungal enlightenment.

The sage color on the binding of a paperback, *Northern Passages: Reflections from Lake Superior Country* caught my eye. A quick read through some of the prose showed that its author, Michael Van Stappen, had written about his Lake Superior country wanderings with scientific and sensual intelligence. Van Stappen had been to Outer Island, the one that reaches farthest out into the lake and is the most difficult to visit. He described that "By virtue of its location, Outer acts like a great convex lens, gathering wayward birds from a wide expanse over the lake." He'd watched the autumn migration of hundreds of species when he helped in a national bird count and had walked the hidden parts of the most remote and exotic island that I might never experience. DJ was already leaning on the counter where he'd placed a *Mad Magazine* anthology. When I added my selections to DJ's, Steve said, "Michael died pretty young—brain cancer. Left a wife and two kids. Loved the area; he could write."

I touched the book's sage cover, which suddenly seemed more precious, then paid. We chatted about our day, and it was then that Steve gave us directions to the ice caves but concurrently offered up his admonition about stepping on the ice. We left the store and felt the winter-softening sunshine reducing some of the snow into rivulets and puddles in the streets, tire ruts, and walkways.

DJ held up a palm to the sunshine. "You're not taking me back on that lake."

"No, I don't think so. But the path to the ice caves is a place to hike."

The warm day, of course, hadn't cleared away the four- and five-foot snow piles. It only shrunk them a few inches. The northern land still appeared in evergreen and white as we followed Highway 13 through Redcliff toward the town of Cornucopia.

Meyer's Lake Road led to a parking area. From the lot, a wide trail to the lakefront, and an opening into the forest revealed a footpath. Scattered footprints served as a trail. A park ranger waited in the lot and walked to our car as soon as our doors opened. "You planning on visiting the caves?"

For a moment, I thought he was going to give us directions. When I answered that we weren't sure if the ice was safe, the ranger was clear and mimicked the voice recording I'd heard early in the morning: "We do not recommend going on the ice today." He added that the way the wind was moving in, the ice could break up, and if we didn't fall into the lake, we could be carried out on an ice floe. After the ranger left and we walked to the forest path, DJ reminded me about the Lake Erie ice fishers who recently made the news when more than fifteen of them had to be rescued from an ice floe that carried them out to open water.

Trees that crowded the path helped us up and down the slopping terraces of the mixed forest. We'd grab the trunks to pull ourselves up and hold on to find safe footing during descent. Our path didn't look like an actual trail; we added to a few sets of footprints while winding through the trees.

This northern part of Wisconsin (and the entire lateral eastern US near the same latitude) marks the southernmost border of the boreal forest and the northernmost border of the mixed hardwood forest. Birch, hemlock, and white pine dominated in these woods—a part of the twelve miles of shoreline designated as the mainland portion of the Apostle Islands National Lakeshore. The forest here included lots of white birch and some yellow birch. The yellow had once dominated the forests. Large tracts of old-growth yellow birch don't remain anymore in Wisconsin except on the Menominee Indian Reservation, where they have been managed for generations with selective harvesting to preserve the integrity of the species and its ecosystem. Around the time I was born, a baby furniture company cut the last forest of yellow birch from the Apostles.

When I skimmed Van Stappen's book back in Bayfield, I'd learned that half the world's forests are now gone, so the forest land we walked seemed doubly important. The woodland stands of yellow birch, hemlock, and white pine once swept in a nearly continuous track all the way to New England. Just east of the Bayfield area, Michigan's Porcupine Mountains still hold tens of thousands of acres of old growth that includes the yellow birch, hemlock, and white pine. Paper birch pop up quickly after a forest fire or cutting; yellow birch take more time to establish themselves and produce sturdier lumber. Some of the old broken trunks of yellow birch we passed were stained crimson, and we were confused by the unexpected color. Eventually, I realized that the windswept cliffs of red sandstone had imprinted their granules on the porous surface of the deteriorating bark. The red-painted, broken trunks of the yellow birch called attention to themselves and to the fact that the forest wasn't quite as it should be. The forest was full but not restored.

DJ stopped under a snowy hemlock branch and looked up, waiting for a breeze to loose the snow on him. While he waited, I perked my ears to sounds of overlapping musical rattles. I followed the bird songs to the side of the ravine we'd just descended. My eyes worked to see the forest inhabitants and after a few moments the brown and tawny patches of three snow buntings appeared as if they had come out of hiding, although they had not moved. They breed farther north than any other land bird and migrate south, relatively speaking, for winter. The first time I saw one, it appeared in our backyard foraging under the feeder with the juncos. I hadn't known this species that looks like a whitish sparrow, but our university extension service helped me identify the buntings during an excited phone call. I wondered what those birds had known as they flew over Canada and hundreds of miles of Lake Superior water, and I wondered how they felt when they finally arrived in these acres of forest, their winter retreat at the end of their migration. And I noticed they were watching us.

DJ was still waiting for snow to fall from the hemlock. I took the snowshoe pole I'd been using as a walking stick and undercut the branch enough to dislodge a big glob of wet snow on his head. "Hey!" He turned around and smiled at me.

"Sorry. I couldn't resist."

I handed him binoculars so he could look at the buntings, which he did without comment. He agreed with me when I suggested we look for tracks, and within fifty feet, we found deer and big rabbit tracks—probably a snowshoe hare.

At the bottom of a ravine, a pair of logs crossed over an awakening brook. When pioneers had no choice but to walk across streams in cold weather, they threw their shoes across the water and walked through, cold-footing it to their dry shoes. Before I had time to caution DJ or find another route, he strolled his lanky limbs across the log and hopped off to the other side of the stream. My ankle, which I had broken years ago, decided to stiffen as soon as I concentrated on slow, precise steps.

I should have known that my starchy caution was a mistake. Walking is an activity the nervous system handles by broad cranial impulses, firing bundles of nerves to stimulate multiple coordinated muscle movements. Brain imaging of people walking shows that most of the measured cranial activity is related to sensory processing—not to the effort of walking. My body and nervous system are wired to walk without much thought devoted to the required motions. A walker's brain is free to think about other things—a fact the ancient Romans understood before the availability of brain wave imaging. A Latin proverb declared centuries ago, *Solvitur Ambulando*, "It is solved by walking." When I became hyper-aware of each precarious step on the icy log, of course, I fell.

While straddling the log, I did what I always do. After any wrong turn on the road, or a fall, or even when I'm lost in an office complex, I imagine there's something I'm supposed to see from the unanticipated angle or location. That way I can pretend there's a reason for the mishap beyond my klutziness or confusion. So, while one foot rested on the boulder that had saved my foot from a soaking, I looked downstream to see the creek widen and turn enough to frame a view of snow-covered rocks mixed with moss-covered rocks. Water washed tenderly around the boulders in this stream. Things would get rougher during the big spring thaw. Even though many of the exposed rocks were rounded and smoothed by the influence of centuries of melt water, the rock my foot rested on was deeply gouged from one end to the other. Scars like this are imbedded on every island and every lakeshore all around Lake Superior. Long before the glacial erosion and melting that formed all the Great Lakes and scarred the rocks and lands, a different form of violence initiated the events that would create the lake basin. Superior is the only Great Lake with a volcanic history.

About 2.7 million years ago, the Mid-Continent Rift split the earth from Thunder Bay Ontario to Kansas. The deepest part of the rift, 1,250 miles, became the depression for the first Great Lake. Active volcanoes ejected cinder, ash, and lava to form a lake basin of basalt and gabbro rocks.

Layers of shale and sandstone built up upon the dense base and between the layers in cracks in the lava. Pockets of pure copper and silver accumulated in gas bubbles. The level of the old lake was 600 feet higher than the present lake that was reshaped by glacial action at the time the other four Great Lakes formed. A broken circle of bluffs around the lake advertised the ancient, lofty shoreline. The old volcanic rock under the sedimentary rock is so dense that the earth's gravity is stronger over the basalt filled rift. Everything and everyone in the Lake Superior region are pulled to the land with a little more force than on most other areas of the planet.

We moved on, and when DJ passed under snow-laden boughs, he paused. I took advantage of the motionless waiting time by looking more intently at our surroundings. Bushes and bark showed chew marks over two feet above the current snow floor. As the snow accumulated, rabbits and hares were able to reach higher branches. While it seemed obvious as I looked, I'd never realized before how the accumulated snow helped them find new food sources.

I waited for a chickadee to fly off the branch before I smacked the limb and another load of snow tumbled down DJ's back. We looked for more tracks. Some were too old and muddled to identify. Round, indistinct circles left a wandering line from some sort of paw. Three-inch circles encased what we thought looked like the impressions of four toes, perhaps a bobcat. We thought we saw a wolf print, but it could have been a dog's. At a sharp summit, distant voices renewed my excitement about possibly seeing the caves.

One more ravine and we'd be at the shoreline. DJ put his arms out like he had when he'd been a fourth-grade school-crossing cadet. "Mom, there's another log bridge—a skinny log—and we are not walking on the lake." He went on about the broken blue ice on Madeline and stranded fishermen in Lake Erie. He pulled in his extended arms, crossed them with defiance and ended with a comment, I'm sure he meant with love, about me not being too light on my feet.

He was right, and I told him so. I don't think I'd have gone on the ice after the ranger told us not to, but I stayed low-key about my agreement, not wanting to deflate the authority of his good decision. Nonetheless, if we saw the owners of those voices and they were heading out to or coming back from viewing the icy layers of castellated stalactites, I would have been tempted.

As soon as we turned back, we began to lose our footing on the iced-over trail. The snow crust that had supported us earlier in the day intermittently collapsed under our weight, our feet plunging through a foot of soggy snow. The trail hugged the curve of the steep land. Once we realized that the outer edge of the path was collapsing, we stepped cautiously toward the inside edges. Watching for tracks as we walked, I came across a familiar print that DJ had made once before in our yard by pushing the pinky side of his fist into the snow and adding five-finger print dots for little toes. I hadn't seen him make these prints on our way out. I inspected the drama DJ had created with manufactured tracks. "Looks like some strange animal."

"Yes, very odd."

"Almost human."

DJ tapped his chin. "But not quite."

Bending down in exaggerated investigational interest, I followed the tracks. "They look like baby footprints, but a barefoot baby could never survive out here."

"Must be some animal with almost-human feet."

"Like, um, Bigfoot? A baby Sasquatch? The tracks end here by these huge raptor prints." DJ had reproduced the owl tracks he'd seen for the first time last month. He walked over and stood with me as we both studied the scene on forest floor. We shook our heads in agreement after I concluded, "I think an owl carried away baby Bigfoot."

The walk back seemed to go much faster, and soon we approached a steep descent we remembered as an ascent from the beginning of the trail. DJ's feet went out from under him, and he slid down on his butt and landed safely at the bottom. He turned around and looked at me, but not for comfort as he used to. This time, he was worried about me. I tied my scarf around my tush, sat down, and watched his amused face as I pushed myself to slide down the hill. He reached for my hand to help me up, "You're weird, Mom."

Instead of heading to the car, I turned to the wide trail that led to the lakeshore. I had to assure DJ that this part of the lake had a beach, and we would not try to walk on the ice. "I just want to try to get a glimpse of the caves with our binoculars."

The wind whipped over the lake and around us. We buttoned up and pulled out gloves and hats from our pockets. A line of sculptured frozen waves lined the intersection of land and water. We walked a half mile toward the caves until just before the beach narrowed to nothing. The red cliffs seemed so close, and I willed myself to see some caves or formations, but the bluff gave up only subtle striations of white that might have decorated the pillars and caverns that were out of reach to us.

I handed the binoculars over to DJ. White islands in the white sea, Eagle, Sand, and York, all sat in the gray horizon. We didn't know these islands, this land, or this water very well. This was only our second time along the National Lakeshore. I knew there was some talk about building a walkway with guard rails to the ice caves to make the path safer, but also concern that if the trip were too easy, people would be more tempted to go out when the winds and ice were dangerous.

I didn't know then, when I stood behind my son and tight-fisted my collar around my shortened neck, what I would discover later that night, after we'd soaked in a hot tub, ate fish and warm soup, crawled between the covers of our own beds, and opened our books. Van Stappen's words kept me awake for hours. His pages transmitted passion for this land and water, the fun and madness he felt jumping waves to keep the breakers out of his boots while fishing in the surf, and the ongoing awareness he experienced as he wandered this northern country. He shared his journey of discovery that began in a store owned by Steve Dunker. In Van Stappen's essay "Old Copper," he described how he had been browsing the natural history section of a used bookstore when Steve showed him a piece of copper and enticed him, questioning him about what he thought it was. He didn't know. It turned out the adze head was an artifact of Old Copper Culture that a treasure hunter with a metal detector found somewhere nearby. Van Stappen discerned a connection while holding this link to those who lived perhaps 7,000 years ago, yet had the ability to fashion metal into tools. These were thought to be the first people, *Homo sapiens* who evolved only after their ancestors climbed down from the trees and learned to walk on two legs and become human. When they began to walk upright, their hands were free to carry babies, fashion tools, hunt with weapons, and carry possessions as they walked to new lands. They crossed the open corridor land bridge, which snaked between glaciers from Asia to Alaska to Canada and all the way to the southern shores of Lake Superior. This land—this natural community—became their home. Van Stappen began to stalk the landscape for clues about the natural history of the area and the people before the Europeans, Ojibwe, and Lakota: the people of the Copper Age whose existence is barely recognized on this continent and whose early history is hidden in a few shards of copper beneath sediment, rocks, and water. Steve had sent Van Stappen on an adventure that would never satisfy his longing to see more and to understand that which was so hidden in the deep recesses of the land. He'd sent Van Stappen on a series of walks. I read Van Stappen's words, "…how do you explain what changes inside you when you lay a hand on a billion-year-old slab of sandstone and feel the sweep of all those years? When you see a chickadee and realize it is looking back at you." I understood what he could not explain. I understood that the walking and sensory interaction, not the drama of the ice caves but the intercourse with the land, was an experience that Steve had pushed us all toward. DJ and I had been sent on a simple journey—a trail we could follow on every attempt to see the caves. As tourists, we'd never come to know the entire Lake Superior region, but we might learn these woods and ravines. We could come back in spring to see the wild orchids and fawns or to the flourish of any season. We could come to feel a kinship, if not with the entire region, then with a few miles of rewilded northern woods.

Van Stappen published one book of prose before he died, and on every page, he implicitly equated a human desire to connect with the natural world with the whale that must surface for air. Every step and every word about the journeys were as Henry David Thoreau said in *Walking*, "a sort of crusade, preached by some Peter the Hermit in us." I know this is not true for everyone. But we who are drawn outdoors are trying to understand the community to which we belong; we are seeking spiritual awe; we are hunting wholeness. This is why we walk.

But that realization came later, after DJ had looked toward the crimson bluff and said, "Maybe next time." We didn't see the caves. We didn't take the big risk. We didn't conquer anything. We only left the city and the pavement without a ticket to an event. I wasn't thinking then about Steve, who sent us here, or Van Stappen, who spent many of his precious years loving this land, when DJ lowered the binoculars as we turned away from the wind and the bluff. Our thoughts were full, not of our steps, but of the next time we would come, without asking directions, to the National Lakeshore and the ice caves.

GOING IN

"When the fruit is ripe, it falls."
RALPH WALDO EMERSON

The setting was all wrong for a farm. As soon as we found the parking lot and saw the inviolate lake rimmed with meadows and distinct little forest plots looking much like the sketch John Muir had made of Fountain Lake 150 years ago, we noticed that the path around the glacial lake was labeled with an Ice Age Trail marker. This area had at least two strikes against it as far as farming was concerned: one, the soil was influenced by the sand laid down during the time when glacial Lake Wisconsin filled several of the nearby counties; and two, this land had been the terminal moraine of a glacier. When the mile-thick ice melted, it deposited accumulated boulders, stones, and gravel throughout the soil. A farmer could pick every stone from the field each spring, but the next winter's icy upheaval would push up another thick crop.

Daniel Muir, John's father, believed he was led by God to bring his family from Scotland to farm this land in the middle of Wisconsin. If Mr. Muir was seeking a landscape with unique characteristics of interrelated terrestrial plant communities as well as diverse aquatic communities, this was a perfect place to live.

I'd hoped this would be the place to talk with DJ about God. Sometimes these conversations come about naturally, but it's easy to go on about the rituals of Christianity (bedtime prayers, Easter sunrise service, and Christmas carols) without ever really talking about spirituality. Perhaps I was trying to assuage my guilt for all those Sunday mornings spent with the newspaper sorted into rotating stacks while DJ and Paul wrestled and rolled over the crinkling pages. Some Sundays we camped, on others we walked, rode bikes or puttered in the yard. Occasionally, we'd go to church, but we never found one that seemed a good fit. Lately I'd been leaning toward a Unitarian congregation, but hadn't joined because, although I was stimulated by the intellectual searching, I missed the joy of worship I'd known in some Protestant congregations. I wouldn't take my son to a church that institutionalized misogyny, and that prerequisite eliminated most of them. John Muir had a relationship with Christianity that I admired. I hoped the place, a few Muir stories, and some personal insights would lead DJ to share and further develop his own spiritual beliefs. Just as our series of sex talks have increased in complexity as he's matured, it was time to lift God above the birds and bees.

We planned to walk around the thirty-acre lake, but as I removed the key from the ignition, the windshield began to blur beneath a misty rain. DJ didn't look disappointed by the drizzle. In fact, he smiled. "Does this mean we won't be able to walk anymore?"

"I want you to see this almost as much as I want to walk the trail. Muir had a dream for this little lake that he never saw fulfilled, but before we are done, you'll see what he never could."

We'd already hiked at the Leopold Foundation land in the morning, and we really did have a good walk. I'd called earlier in the week and begged to be allowed to join a guided tour, the only way to see the Aldo Leopold land and shack. DJ was the only kid. All the other walkers were over forty and as goofy about Leopold and being able to enter his shack as I was. Every person who has studied conservation since 1949 has built an understanding upon Leopold's land ethic: "A thing is right when it tends to preserve the integrity, stability, and beauty of the biotic community. It is wrong when it tends otherwise." I watched a woman next to me bounce in place, smile wide, and ball up her shaking hands when our guide said we could go into the old chicken coop Leopold had fashioned into a cabin of sorts. She gasped as she crossed the threshold of the famous shack of Leopold's *Sand County Almanac*. One step behind her, I leaned close to her and whispered, "Yippee." She reached back, squeezed my elbow, and pulled me in. It was just a shack, but it was Leopold's. Throughout the hike and tour, DJ silently witnessed the nature nuts identifying plants and birdcalls for each other. The bird calling "Drink your tea eee eee," was a Rufous-sided towhee. The red-sand riverbed showed us where the Wisconsin River had flowed during Leopold's time; it had since meandered 150 yards northeasterly. We all took turns looking at the Dutchman's breeches—a ferny plant with white flowers. DJ was the only one who didn't contort his body to investigate the low-growing flower that looked like upside-down white pantaloons with a narrow yellow waistband. We looked into the bloom, imagining how a bumblebee reached deep into the pantaloon legs to collect the nectar and then withdrew and rolled up its tongue and stowed it beneath a horny sheath under its head. One of the men joked quietly (out of respect for DJ) to his wife about how he had always wondered what learning about the birds and bees had to do with getting into someone's pants. Now he knew.

DJ didn't join in much, except to whisper a few observations to me. Once in the car to Fountain Lake, he napped.

DJ closed his eyes again while I watched the lake through the side window that was shielded from the wind and raindrops. Rays of sun streaked through the clouds and made sparkles of the raindrops sitting on lily pads, grasses, leaves, and the ripples of water. The light reminded me of John Muir's first look at this lake. I took Muir's *The Story of My Boyhood and Youth* out of my backpack and read aloud: "When we first saw Fountain Lake Meadow, on a sultry evening, sprinkled with millions of lightning-bugs throbbing with light, the effect was so strange and beautiful that it seemed far too marvelous to be real. Looking from our shanty on the hill, I thought that the whole wonderful fairy show must be in my eyes: for only in fighting, when my eyes were struck, had I ever seen anything in the least like it."

I reached over and touched DJ's knee. He opened his eyes. "Listen, DJ. Muir caught lightning bugs and brought them in the house to look at them, just like you did last summer. Muir was eleven, exactly your age, when he moved here." Again, DJ did not respond. I sighed and looked at my book. "Here he talks about carrying lighting bugs to the shanty, 'where we watched them throbbing and flashing out their mysterious light at regular intervals, as if each little passionate glow were caused by the beating heart.'"

I touched his knee again. He didn't appear at all interested; in fact, he looked asleep. I couldn't stop myself. He would appreciate this place more if he understood how Muir enjoyed it—at least that's what I told myself so I could enjoy the words again in this place. Even from inside the car, saying the words seemed to consecrate the place. I opened the book: "And listen to this part, about when he and his family first came here,

> 'This sudden plash into pure Wildness—baptism in Nature's warm heart—how utterly happy it made us! Nature streaming into us, wooingly teaching her wonderful glowing lessons, so unlike the dismal grammar ashes and cinders so long thrashed into us. Here without knowing it we still were in school; every wild lesson a love lesson, not whipped but charmed into us. Oh, that glorious Wisconsin wilderness!'"

Muir's joy didn't move DJ. He kept his eyes closed—no reaction. I resorted to guilt. "This is the best Mother's Day gift I could ever ask for, seeing Muir's Fountain Lake with you."

He stretched and opened his eyes. "Are we going to do this or what?"

I grabbed the backpack and opened the car door. "It's only a Scotch mist—not enough to stop us."

"What's a Scotch mist?"

I held out my palm to the sky. "This. Mist you hardly notice." There was enough rain to offer us the scent of fresh spring. Plants and trees release volatile oils that collect on surfaces. Rain reacts with the oils and carries the fragrance as a gas in the air. We didn't breathe in only this perfume. Tiny spores of the actinomycetes bacteria in the soil were also aerosolized by the drizzle. They smell sweet too. These composting bacteria that recycle life are so common all over the world that a fresh smell after rain is nearly universal.

DJ didn't think they'd done much to commemorate Muir at this park.

A granite marker called him the "Father of the National Parks." A wooden sign claimed him as "Wisconsin's adopted son." One more sign at a small boat landing told us about the "no motors" rule when walked to the pier and dipped our hands in the frigid water. That was about the extent of the park's development. Our path divided the land with meadow on one side and an oak opening between us and the lake. This pairing was common when the land was wild. Prairies make dry grasses that are subject to fires; burr oak can withstand a quick prairie fire because of its fire-resistant, cork-like bark. As the sunlight found an opening through the clouds, birdsongs and wild turkey gobbles busied the air.

I stopped. "DJ, listen to all those birds." Whistling yellowthroats fluttered into the oaks. Warblers sang their "sweet sweet" song. A thick-bodied female kingfisher rattled as she left an oak branch and flew into a shaft of sunshine that ignited her fancy blue and white feathers and the chestnut-colored belt across her belly. She stalled and plunged into the lake. Kingfishers dig tunnels for nests and differ from most avian species in that the female is the most colorful of the couple. DJ wondered if the fact that they didn't have to sit on a nest out in the open accounted for their fancier feathers. Different songs from different species began to overlap so thickly it was hard to distinguish one from the other. DJ started to walk, but I held up my hand. "Just wait. I want to listen." Instead of testing myself and priding myself on my identification abilities, I tried to just listen. Muir, no doubt, would have called the singers a choir.

DJ scanned the perimeter of the lake as we continued walking. "Where's his house?"

"It's long gone, but somewhere across the lake, another one stands on exactly the same spot."

"So, this is the place of his happy childhood?"

"Not really. He called his time here his 'years of servitude.'" I explained that his father believed being harsh with his children would lead them to God. Before Muir came to Wisconsin, he knew about three-fourths of the Old Testament and all of the New by heart. In addition to schoolwork, his father gave him memorization assignments, and if he or his siblings didn't know their verses, the child got what Muir called "a sound thrashing."

The Muir children did not attend school once they came to the farm. They worked these fields in summer, each farm day a hard sweaty day of about sixteen or seventeen hours. Even though dead wood laid on the ground in abundance, Mr. Muir would pull the logs from cleared land into piles to rot while the house, heated in winter by only a kitchen stove, would be so cold the family's standing water and wet clothes would freeze in the cabin. The family often had to beat their frozen socks to make them wearable after the sweat from the previous day's work had made them icy stiff. Mr. Muir wouldn't let young Johnny or the other children read anything except the Bible, and he gave them only two days a year off from work, Christmas and the Fourth of July. Some say John had every Sunday off, but he complained that church time, Sunday school, and Bible study took away more than half of the day. Days off always included tending to the animals. When John was older and was asked to teach Sunday school, he said he would if he could do it his way. At a time when most farmers saw critters and varmints as either food or competition for food, John Muir saw the animals and land as a lesson in God's care. So, he held his Sunday school classes outdoors.

I reached into my backpack for Muir's book and read. "One touch of nature makes the whole world kin; and it is truly wonderful how love-telling the small voices of these birds are, how far they reach through the woods into one another's hearts and into ours."

DJ kept walking and looked over his shoulder at me. "Oh, he sounds like a real riot."

"Okay, I'll put the books away for now." Muir's joy was so exuberant that I could see how uncool his words must have seemed to an adolescent, but I loved Muir's intelligence, unselfconsciousness, and enthusiasm. His passion always felt authentic.

DJ pointed to the ground. "Pine moss." Then, just as suddenly, he said, "Remember in the movie *Hot Shots* when all the people jump out of the plane and yell 'Geronimo,' then the guy in the feathers and war paint jumps out and yells, 'Me'?" He kept talking. "The best part of *The Two Towers* is when Sméagol brings back the two skinny rabbits. Sam wants to make stew with them and says, 'What we need is a few good taters,' and

Sméagol wonders, 'What's Taters?' Sam says, '*Po-ta-toes*! Boil 'em, mash 'em, stick 'em in a stew.'"

When he started singing a song about an albino black sheep, I found myself tuning out. I was amused, yet couldn't stay interested in DJ's conversation any better than he could stay interested in mine. He'd been contained and respectful all morning, but now he was hiking in drizzle that had picked up. He looked and sounded happy. Muir would love knowing a carefree child was walking around his lake.

While his father pounded religion into his son, Muir developed a love for the God he met in the fields, woods, and later in the mountains of California and wild places around the world. He knew that the book of 1 John says "God is Love," and he experienced the matrix of the wilderness as divine. He became a scientist, making geologic and botanical discoveries, a writer who created a fresh dialect of nature writing (nobody had ever been so joyful in the wilderness). His relationship with God developed from his understanding of Christianity, his attentiveness to evidence of God, and his maturing mind. Many Christians, including his father, saw his scientific interest as a proud attempt to explain that which should be accepted without question as the creation of an omnipotent God. Calvinists and Puritans tended to see wilderness as a symbol of chaotic godlessness, but that idea didn't square with Muir, who knew his Bible better than most ardent churchgoers. Thinking was always a part of his religion. Evolutionists took issue with Muir's insistence that Nature was infused with an underlying quality of benevolence that could be experienced when one looked for the overall harmony in the natural world. Muir said, "No pain here, no dull empty hours, no fear of the past, no fear of the future. These blessed mountains are so compactly filled with God's beauty, no petty personal hope or experience has room to be." Muir came to see the creation in nature's violence and the life born of every death. Seeing the wilderness in terms much larger than his own comfort, his own profit, and even his life granted him access to a communion with nature that became the center of his spirituality. He accepted the concept of evolution, but his mind was open enough to believe that understanding natural or scientific processes did not limit the idea of God as creator. Scientific revelations offered glimpses into God's intricacies. Nature was the soul of God. My thoughts had distracted me, and I hadn't noticed that DJ had quieted down. Sensing an opening, I asked him to tell me about his thoughts about God.

"Ma'oom," he keened, "I believe what you believe."

"Can you explain?"

He exhaled, excessively. "Jesus died for our sins. We're supposed to pray, be thankful, treat others nice even if they don't think like we do, and we should respect all God's creation."

The words came from his memory, but it was, I thought, a good answer.

He noticed the edge of an oak opening and pointed to a wide meadow. "Can we go over there?"

"I think we should stay on the trail. There's a prairie restoration project at the base of that hill on what once was a farm field or maybe an animal corral or pasture. I don't want to trample anything." DJ raised his binoculars to his eyes, and in anticipation, I did the same.

"Did you see something?" I asked.

"Just grass moving around, but something whistled. Listen."

The call soon identified itself. The "bob white, bob bob white" whistle carried through the air—not loudly but as if it were transmitted in high fidelity. "Northern Bobwhite quail," I said. "I read that a bunch of them were released here in the eighties to help them reestablish in the area."

We waited until the male ran into a clearing and we saw his thick white eyebrow stripes. This bird is not a great flier and isn't migratory, characteristics that make it easy to find. Its varied diet includes foods found all around the lake: pine seeds, acorn, thistle, and even poison ivy. Additionally, quail are good eating. At one time, they were hunted out of the area.

It was too early in the season to see much more than last year's dried grass in the meadows, building material for the birds' nests. At first glance everything was tan, but after a time, we came to see a variety of textures in the bronzed foliage that told a tale of diverse plant life. These tough stems and blades protected the nests of the meadow birds and still held seed pods to feed the nesting families. Spring rabbits, moles, snakes, and more also used these dried grasses as shelter for their young families.

DJ shielded his eyes with his hand. "Where's the house?"

I didn't know. DJ seemed interested in these meadows, so I told him about Muir's favorite horse. Nob worked these meadows when they were fields. She was a smart mare and could learn almost anything. Muir called her the stoutest, gentlest, bravest little horse he ever saw. Once, she'd been stolen and was missing for months, until the family saw a newspaper notice that she'd been recovered from the thief. While other horses got skittish during lightning or around snakes, Nob feared nothing, or almost nothing. She stood stock still whenever she went near the site where she'd been stolen away, so vexed that she trembled. Her heartbeats were so loud that Muir said when he sat on her back, he heard "*boomp, boomp, boomp,* like the drumming of a partridge."

One sweltering summer day, Mr. Muir rode Nob into Portage and rode her back very hard so that he wouldn't be late for a revival meeting. Mr. Muir got to his church meeting, but Nob didn't recover. They left her untethered in her final days, and she tried to follow the children who had been her work and playmates. Muir said it was awfully touching. She came to him trembling, hemorrhaging, wheezing, and she looked into Muir's eyes. The teenage Muir tried to soothe her and bathed her head, but she lay down, gasped, and died. The family gathered around their faithful helpmate and wept.

DJ kept looking out to the field. "So Muir blamed his father?"

"He was careful not to blame his dad directly. There certainly could have been something else wrong with the horse. Muir said the 'whole family' cried when she died, so I guess that meant the dad too. But Muir recognized animals as fellow mortals and didn't believe in a God in heaven urging anyone to drive a horse as if it had no soul, no rights, and existed only to serve a human master. Nature gave Muir a look at God he could understand, one that seemed consistent with the loving and sacrificial Jesus of the Bible. Muir found God in nature, not in the sermons of his father. Muir once said, 'I only went out for a walk, and finally concluded to stay out till sundown, for going out, I found, was really going in.'"

DJ wondered if young Muir ever got another horse. He did; he grew up to own a fruit orchard in California and was known to fire any worker who was cruel to an animal.

After we'd walked a few hundred yards in silence, DJ said, "Going in. He meant, like knowing yourself." He saw me raise my eyebrows, impressed by his insight, but before I could say anything, he began quoting from the movie *Napoleon Dynamite*, about how "Chicks dig guys with skills."

The soil darkened and grew springier when we entered a fen with a creek running through it. This boggy soil was further along in its spring development than the prairies. Marsh marigolds pointed their yellow blooms toward a spring creek. Tiny fiddleheads showed graduated states of uncurled fern leaves, and the rare ecosystem that supported the threatened flora delineated its borders by being the greenest patch of land we'd seen near the lake. Muir wrote about this fen to his brother-in-law, who later lived here, asking him to save the property, or at least the little bog—for the sake of the ferns and flowers. The brother-in-law wouldn't sell the place to Muir, who only wanted the place to be allowed its wildness. When Muir came back for a visit, eighteen years after he left, the meadow sod was broken by grazing cattle, but the bog by the lake still grew orchids, ferns, and wildflowers, and it flourished next to the flowering pond lilies of the lake. Twenty years later, when Muir saw the place again for the last time, even the little bog was trampled away. The sandy soil here never did yield high crops after the initial topsoil, which took over 10,000 years to accumulate, was worn away in a few seasons of farming. Eventually, the land was left fallow. By the 1950s, the fields had rested a few decades. With its pockets of tamarack, rich fen, open bog, wet mesic prairie, high mesic prairie, and dry forest, the land began to attract the interest of naturalists. Over the years, governmental and private organizations have been buying up and protecting bits of the original property and adjacent land.

On a simple wooden bridge that spanned a little creek, we spotted a house on a hill. Through binoculars, we saw some sort of memorial plaque, but couldn't read it. I said I thought it was the house, because it seemed to be in the right place, and the plaque would make sense because the eighty acres of original Muir land were named a National Historic Landmark. Erik Brynildson, a landscape architect/ecologist who specialized in native landscape restoration, owned a few acres containing and surrounding the site of the old home. Very near the home site a little burr oak shanty used to stand; it was the shack that Muir lived in before they built the big house. Young John would sit on top of the roof and watch the courting cranes and the currents of passenger pigeons. The great flocks of pigeons were gone, but Muir did see some of what he called the "bonnie bird" with a "fine rosy breast." He'd read Audubon's account of passenger pigeon flocks so large they darkened the sky for as far as the eye could see. Audubon saw the low-flying birds beat down with shovels and then sold for a penny a piece or even fed to the hogs. Muir lived long enough to know that the very last passenger pigeon died in the Cincinnati Zoo in November of 1914. That same year, he lost a battle to save the Hetch Hetchy Valley, which he called the Little Sierra. He tried with his writing and every bit of influence he had to stop the decision to flood the California valley as a reservoir, but just before his death, he knew he'd lost.

I led as we crossed the little bridge and walked toward a mixed wood where the path in the open woods was widened. DJ moved up to my side. He wanted to know if present-day Fountain Lake looked as it had when Muir was a little boy.

"No, but it's much more beautiful than when he last visited and saw all the land trampled by grazing." The passenger pigeon will never be back, but we knew the turkey and bobwhite had returned. Plants like wild rice, lady's slipper, and cranberry were all extirpated from this area. They could be reintroduced, but we would all have to careful not to trample them again. The last I'd heard, Brynildson was trying to reestablish the prairie grouse. Loons sometimes stop during migration, but none had taken up residency. I thought Muir would be heartened by the progress and the influence of his words in still motivating people toward restoration efforts, but he surely would be shaken by the enormity of the destruction to the earth's ecosystems.

Muir's spirituality was about a personal relationship with a God he met in nature. DJ stayed quiet while I explained my view of Christianity. Jesus is a personal savior, and therefore, everyone's relationship with God is a little different. No one can interpret God completely for another. Scripture can hold different meanings for each reader. I believe that when people stop thinking and group together to follow a singular and rigid interpretation of sacred texts, they are often manipulated and exploited. Jesus spoke in parables, because story has depth and requires thoughtful examination before the lesson can be applied.

I had my own view about Communion. Jesus told us to think of Him as often as we eat and drink. To me, that meant our spirituality should be as important and as frequent a part of our life as eating is, and a Communion service is a ritualized version of that nourishment. Many Christians, of course, would consider my interpretation as blasphemy. Years after I came to my own conclusions about the dogmatic trappings of religion, I learned that Emerson gave up his formal ministry because he could not pretend to believe in the mysticism of ceremony.

DJ wanted to know if I was a Christian like Muir, but I thought that Muir's Christianity and wilderness ethic were a bit more muscular than mine. I didn't climb mountains or sleep on rocks. I did admit that I might be as uncool and gushy as Muir. I understood his words: "To make our world like theirs, a shrine, Sink down, oh traveler, on your knees, God stands before you in these trees."

Near the end of our walk, we saw a small line in the grass that looked like a deer trail that led to the lake. DJ asked if we could follow it to the lake, and this time I said, "Yes, if we are careful to stay on the path." The clear kettle lake gave a crystalline view of every stone and every grain of sand in the shallow water near the shore. The bed was formed by a chunk of ice that broke away from a retreating glacier and was buried in the layers of sediment and soil of a new age. When the ice finally melted, it had sculpted a lake.

DJ picked up a handful of stones and threw one. "Know what I liked today?" DJ asked. He talked about our morning on Leopold's land. Our group had gathered at the spot where Leopold had chopped the tree in his essay "The Good Oak."

We'd all stood quietly listening to a reading of the story of the oak that had been felled by lightning. Leopold went out to cut the tree for firewood and sawed into eighty years of growth rings, giving a history of conservation efforts. When he cuts to 1865, the very core of the good oak, Leopold writes about Muir trying to buy his old home farm as a "sanctuary for the wildlife" that had gladdened his youth. I took *Sand Country Almanac* out of my backpack and read Leopold's words again: "1865 still stands in Wisconsin history as the birth year of mercy for things natural, wild, and free."

DJ snickered.

"What's so funny?"

"Just when that lady read that part, a pizza delivery car went by. Don't you remember? Moosehead Pizza."

The image of the huge three-dimensional fiberglass moose head covering an entire car roof came back to me. That stupid head (and maybe Bullwinkle) are the only moose a lot of the kids in Wisconsin have ever seen. The moose have been gone from most of the state since long before Leopold purchased his worn-out land and worked toward its restoration. They were gone even before the Muirs arrived and joined in the creation of the American dream, which was laden with hopes for a liberty that included land ownership and religious freedom. Settlers took up their Christian duty to have dominion over the land with naive abandon. They took. Their survival depended upon cutting forests, killing birds, harnessing water, and trapping mammals for hides, but many were and are unable to make a distinction between survival, comfort, and avarice. They did not, and we still do not, understand that our dominion gives us the power to destroy a species, a landscape, an ecosystem and that this whirlpool of destruction could grow so deep and so wide that we will all be pulled in.

How do we, and how will our children, understand how to have dominion over a natural world when we only know summer nights by the comfort of lying in bed in a sealed room while the air conditioner blows away the feeling of the season? Most of us don't hear the loon call at sunset. We are not accustomed to the baritone gulp of the bullfrogs. We wake behind closed curtains to an alarm, oblivious to songbirds that began their euphony a full hour before the first haze of light blurred the darkness.

Only a few of the faithful celebrate the sensory renewal in the honking of geese and the hum of a hummingbird, "Thank you God for another season," when the migrators arrive and depart on seasonal winds. Last winter I walked by the river every evening, and I never heard the owl's familiar hoot glissade between the snow and the dark sky. Maybe next year. I wonder if tomorrow's children will open their windows and have an understanding of the autochthonous sounds they should hear. If the landscape is mute, will they know that they are hearing death?

Most of us exercise our liberty and push for our American dream of possession by creating an edifice of selfishness in our homes and on our bodies that does not satisfy. If it did, we would by now own our happiness within our pile of possessions.

The standards for beauty, comfort, and success create an artificial and largely indoor world of consumption. We scream when we see a mouse or a bee, and most would rather swim in a pool than a lake. We wear clothes and hairstyles that can't withstand rain or wind. We ask the Department of Natural Resources and the hunters to control and kill the wolves and then complain about too many deer. Fuel economy in cars is only an issue when the price of oil rises—not when the concentration of carbon dioxide in the air rises. We are parenting our children and living our lives without the capacity to have intelligent dominion over the natural world because our lives are unnatural. We don't know what we are doing, and we don't care.

The world population now doubles every forty years. The seven billion people on the earth will have less room per person to live and grow food for every year that they live. The concentration of carbon dioxide in the air has increased from 280 parts per million, before the Industrial Revolution to over 360. The numbers continue to rise and the temperature with it. We are each a portion of the earth, but we place ourselves above the natural world as if we would could exist without a living planet beneath our feet.

DJ threw his last pebble. "So is this what Muir wanted, but never saw? His childhood farm set aside for the birds, plants, and animals?"

I pulled out my book one more time. "When Muir wrote about Fountain Lake, he said he wished it could be protected: 'Even if I should never see it again, the beauty of its lilies and orchids is so pressed into my mind. I shall always enjoy looking back at them in imagination, even across seas and continents, and perhaps after I am dead.'" I told DJ about a glimmer of hope for Muir's Hetch Hetchy, flooded for nearly nine decades. A few years ago, Tom Philip, the editor of the *Sacramento Bee*, won a Pulitzer in editorial writing for a series of articles urging the restoration of Yosemite's Hetch Hetchy Valley. He frequently used Muir's firsthand accounts of the valley to entice the public to consider the hidden marvel and the possibility of resurrection. There is still a scant hope that Muir will win the battle he started over 100 years ago.

DJ squatted and pulled swirls through the water. "It's warmer on this side. If I lived here, I'd swim in these shallows." In 1849, an eleven-year-old Muir felt this water for the first time. He had never lived near a lake before and almost drowned here, but he learned to swim by watching how frogs kick. And he grew to live in harmony with his simple, grand prayers for wild places.

I bent down next to DJ. As we sat on our haunches in the Scotch mist, we bowed our heads and pulled our hands through the clear water and watched the bubbles and currents. DJ scooped up a handful of the lake and stood up. As he rose, most of the water drained from his cupped hand.

BIBLIOGRAPHICAL NOTES

This book is neither a scientific nor a cultural work of scholarship: nonetheless, readings and references did enter the vortex from which these true stories emerged.

Some names and details were changed in writing this book for reasons of privacy.

CHAPTER ONE: BETWEEN LAND AND WATER
1. Emerson, Ralph Waldo, *The Works of Ralph Waldo Emerson, in 12 vols. Fireside Edition*, Vol. 1 Nature, Addresses, and Lectures, Chapter 4, "Language," Boston and New York: 1909. Accessed from http://oll.libertyfund.org/title/1831 on 2009-06-10.

2. Crary, Elizabeth, *I'm Lost*, Parenting Press, Inc., Seattle: 1985.

3. Peterson, Tory, *A Field Guide to the Birds of Eastern and Central North America*, 5th edition, Houghton Mifflin Harcourt, Boston: 2002.

4. Gerard Manley Hopkins, *Poems of Gerard Manley: Now First Published*, 1918, "Spring," Editor: Robert Bridges, EBook #22403. Accessed from http://www.gutenberg.org/files/22403/22403-8.txt on 2009-06-10.

5. Sabin, Edwin Legrand, *Boy's Book of Indian Warriors and Heroic Women*, George W. Jacobs & Co, Philadelphia: 1918.

6. Percy Bysshe Shelley, Quiller-Couch, Arthur Thomas, Sir. *The Oxford Book of English Verse*, "To a Skylark," Oxford, Clarendon: 1919.

CHAPTER TWO: CLOSE TO HOME
1. Eliot, Thomas Sterns, *The Waste Land*, "Death by Water," New York: Boni and Liveright: 1922.

2. Leonardo da Vinci, *The Notebooks of Leonardo Da Vinci*, "Of Life and Death," gutenberg etext# 5000: 1452-1519. Accessed from http://www.gutenberg.org/etext/5000 on 2009-06-10.

3. John Muir, *A Thousand-Mile Walk to the Gulf*, "Chapter 4, Camping among the Tombs," Edited By William Frederic Badè, The Riverside Press, Boston and New York: 1916.

CHAPTER THREE: COUNTY OF ORIGIN
1. Berry, Wendell, *The Unsettling of America: Culture and Agriculture*, San Francisco, Sierra Club Books: 1996.

2. Emerson, Ralph Waldo, *The Works of Ralph Waldo Emerson, in 12 vols. Fireside Edition*, Boston and New York: 1909, Vol. 1 Nature, Addresses, and Lectures, Chapter 5, "Discipline." Accessed from http://oll.libertyfund.org/title/1831 on 2009-06-10.

CHAPTER FOUR: SHEPHERDED FLIGHTS
1. Leopold, Aldo, *Sand County Almanac and Sketches Here and There* (Special Commemorative Edition), Oxford University Press, New York and Oxford: 1987.

2. Thoreau, Henry David, *Excursions In Field And Forest*, Etext 9846, 1863. Accessed from http://www.gutenberg.org/etext/9846, on 2009-06-13.

CHAPTER FIVE: VALLEY OF THE SNAKE
1. Roosevelt, Eleanor, *In Your Hands* Speech: *A Guide for Community Action for the Tenth Anniversary of the Universal Declaration of Human Rights*." March 27, 1958, United Nations, New York. Accessed from http://www.udhr.org/history/frbioer.htm, 2009-06-13.

2. Carson, Rachel, *Silent Spring*, Houghton Mifflin, Boston: 1962.

3. C.S. Lewis, *The Abolition of Man*, HarperOne, New York: 2001.

4. Kozol, Jonathan, *Amazing Grace: Lives of Children and the Conscience of a Nation*, Harper Collins, New York: 2002.

5. Scott Russell Sanders, *Writing From the Center*, Indiana University Press, Bloomington: 1997.

6. Wordsworth, William, *Poems in Two Volumes, Volume One*: 1770-1850, "Composed on a Westminster Bridge," Project Gutenberg. Accessed from http://infomotions.com/etexts/gutenberg/dirs/etext05/pwdw110.htm on 2009-06-11.

7. George Crandall quote on state plaque, verified, Stewards of the Dells of the Wisconsin River, Inc., Wisconsin Dells on 2009-06-11.

CHAPTER SIX: STILL AUTUMN
1. Sir Walter Scott, *Marmion: A Tale of Flodden Field by Walter Scott*, 1808 Fullbooks. Accessed http://www.fullbooks.com/Marmion—A-Tale-of-Flodden-Field1.html on 2009-06-11.

2. Wordsworth, William, *Poems in Two Volumes, Volume 1*, "The Redbreast Chasing the Butterfly:"1802, Project Gutenberg, Zielinska, Marie: translator. Accessed from http://infomotions.com/etexts/gutenberg/dirs/etext05/pwdw110.htm on 2009-06-11.

3. Frost, Robert, *A Boy's Will*, "Reluctance," New York: Henry Holt and Company: 1915.

4. Whitman, Walt, *Leaves of Grass*, "Song of the Open Road," Philadelphia: David McKay, [c1900], accessed http://www.gutenberg.org/ebooks/1322 on 2009-06-11.

CHAPTER SEVEN: EAGLE WATCHING
Morrison, Tony, "The Dancing Mind," National Book Awards Acceptance Speech, November 6, 1996.

CHAPTER EIGHT: THE POINT OF FEBRUARY
1. Carson, Rachel, *The Sense of Wonder*, New York, Harper Collins Publishers Inc.: 1998.

2. Neihardt, John, G., *Black Elk Speaks: As Told to John G. Neihardt*, Lincoln, University of Nebraska Press: 1972.

CHAPTER NINE: SECOND DATE WITH THE APOSTLES
1. Leopold, Aldo, *Sand County Almanac and Sketches Here and There* (Special Commemorative Edition), Oxford University Press, New York and Oxford: 1987.

2. Van Stappen, Michael, *Northern Passages: Reflections from Lake Superior Country*, Madison, Wisconsin, Prairie Oak Press: 1998.

3. Thoreau, Henry David, *Walking*, EBook #1022: 1862. Accessed at http://www.gutenberg.org/etext/1022, on 2009-6-11.

CHAPTER TEN: GOING IN
1. Emerson, Ralph Waldo, *Essays by Ralph Waldo Emerson: Spiritual Laws*: 1803-1882, http://www.gutenberg.org/ebooks/16643 on 2009-06-13.

2. Muir, John, *The Story of my Boyhood and Youth*: 1913, http://www.sierraclub.org/john_muir_exhibit/frameindex.html?http://www.sierraclub.org/John_Muir_Exhibit/writings/the_story_of_my_boyhood_and_youth/, 2009-06-13.

3. Leopold, Aldo, *Sand County Almanac and Sketches Here and There* (Special Commemorative Edition), Oxford University Press, New York and Oxford: 1987.

ABOUT THE AUTHOR

Amy Lou Jenkins is a writer, speaker, nurse, and educator from Wisconsin. Her writing has been honored by the Wisconsin Jade Ring Award, X.J. Kennedy Award for Nonfiction, *Florida Review* Editor Award in Creative Nonfiction, *Flint Hills Review* Nonfiction Award, Ellis/Henderson Outdoor Writing Award, and *Literal Latté* Annual Essay Award. She is the recipient of a Mesa Refuge Writing Fellowship and has taught writing at Carroll University and in many writing workshops, conferences, and classes. Her work has appeared in multiple magazines, newspapers, and anthologies including *Wisconsin Academy Review, Flint Hills Review, Milwaukee Journal Sentinel, Shepherds Express, Florida Review, Inkpot, Earth Island Journal, Generations, Rosebud, Big Apple Parent, MetroParent, Washington Families, Sport Literate,* Chicken Soup, Cup of Comfort books, *Women on Writing, Wild with Child* and *The Maternal is Political.* Amy Lou lives in the Milwaukee area with her husband, son, and two spoiled dogs. Follow her at www.AmyLouJenkins.com.